Developing
Professional Skills:
PROPERTY

Colleen E. Medill
Warren R. Wise Professor of Law
University of Nebraska College of Law

WEST®

MAT # 41164905

© 2012 Thomson Reuters
610 Opperman Drive
St. Paul, MN 55123
1-800-313-9378

Printed in the United States of America

ISBN: 9-780-314-27625-4

This book is dedicated to
Rose, Kathleen, Josie, and Matthew

Preface

LAW SCHOOLS TODAY aspire to teach professional legal skills. The current emphasis on skills training is in response to the criticism that the traditional law school curriculum does not adequately train students to practice law. The high cost of law school tuition, coupled with the tight job market for law school graduates in recent years, has intensified the demand for more skills training in law schools.

Incorporating skills training into doctrinal law courses is challenging. This is particularly true for law school courses that are taught during the first year of law school. Elaborate simulations can crowd out the coverage of fundamental legal concepts and doctrines, leaving both the professor and the students frustrated. The professor feels that there is never enough time adequately to cover the subject matter. The students feel that there is never enough time, period.

Developing Professional Skills: Property is designed to provide skills training to law students in a time-efficient manner. Each chapter in this book focuses on one of the following four core legal skills:

▶ Client Counseling (including engagement of a new client, interviewing and fact gathering);

- Legal Drafting (including client correspondence via letters and e-mails as well as traditional legal document drafting);

- Negotiation; and

- Advocacy.

Students are expected to spend about one to two hours outside of the classroom preparing the skills assignment for each chapter. A comprehensive Teacher's Manual gives the professor both guidance and discretion in determining how much classroom discussion time to devote to the material in each chapter. The professor may spend a brief amount of time reviewing the "answer" to the problem presented in the chapter. Or, the professor may expand the discussion to include concepts of professional responsibility and the norms of modern legal practice. Suggestions for incorporating professional responsibility concepts and the norms of legal practice into the classroom discussion are contained in the Teacher's Manual. For professors who desire to expand the scope of a skills exercise, selected provisions of the *Model Rules of Professional Conduct* and client time sheets are reproduced as Appendix material at the end of the book.

Developing Professional Skills: Property is intended to make the introductory Property course fun for the students. The standard classroom routine of reading cases and answering questions generally is not what students envision when they enter law school. As attorneys, students will encounter idiosyncratic, demanding, and occasionally unreasonable clients, constantly evolving new technology, old-fashioned financial and time management constraints, and most of all, interesting problems to solve. Although no book can truly simulate the nuanced tapestry that is modern legal practice, the skills exercises in this book can be used to enhance and enrich the students' educational experience.

Several generous friends provided support and willingly shared their expertise to assist me in the creation of this book. First and foremost,

I thank Louis Higgins, Editor In Chief at West Academic Publishing, for his unwavering enthusiasm for this project. Dean Susan Poser and the University of Nebraska College of Law provided both expertise and financial support for this project. Professor Kristen Blankley at the University of Nebraska College of Law shared her knowledge and experience for the chapters involving negotiation skills. Associate Dean Glenda Pierce at the University of Nebraska College of Law provided assistance with designing the chapters involving advocacy skills. Professor Joan MacLeod Heminway at The University of Tennessee College of Law provided guidance concerning the practical points of corporate securities law. Finally, Professor Michelle Harner at the University of Maryland School of Law answered all of my questions concerning the *Model Rules of Professional Conduct* and generously shared her experiences teaching professional responsibility to first year law students.

Colleen E. Medill
September 1, 2011

Introduction

Developing Professional Skills: Property introduces you to the variety of skills that differentiate the law student from the experienced legal practitioner. Like any type of skill, acquiring professional legal skills takes time and patience. Most of all, it takes practice. Each chapter in this book provides you with the opportunity to practice a legal skill that you are likely to use again and again after you graduate from law school.

The chapters of this book are organized according to topics that usually are covered in an introductory Property course. In Chapter One, you will reply to a client's e-mail question concerning who has the superior right to possession of found personal property. Chapter Two requires you to write a letter to an opposing party who claims title to a portion of your client's land based on adverse possession. In Chapter Three, you must counsel an elderly client who wants to avoid probate by making lifetime gifts. Chapter Four requires you to summarize in writing the legal and practical issues that may arise if your client conveys away a defeasible present interest in real property. You also will prepare the language of a deed that conveys a defeasible present interest. In Chapter Five, you will interview a group of new clients who desire to acquire a commercial investment property as co-owners. Chapter Six involves the negotiation of the terms of a commercial lease. In Chapter Seven, you will craft the major points for a brief in support of claims for fraudulent misrepresentation and failure to disclose latent defects related to your client's new home. Chapter Eight shows you how to draft various types of deeds. In Chapter Nine, you will draft an easement agreement for a billboard sign. Finally, in Chapter Ten you will negotiate the compensation due to a property owner whose land is being taken for a road improvement project.

Client counseling, legal drafting, negotiation and advocacy are the core skills of the legal profession. *Developing Professional Skills: Property* provides you with the opportunity to begin to acquire these skills.

Table of Contents

CHAPTER ONE

Possession Rights to Found Property
The Watch and the Worker

THE BARGAIN STORE is an established client of your law firm. The Bargain Store's owner, Lea Smith, is no longer actively involved in the day-to-day operation of the business and relies on the company's general manager, Jack Riley, to oversee operations at the store's retail locations. Rather than hourly billing, the Bargain Store pays a monthly retainer fee to your firm so that Jack can consult with the firm's attorneys on routine legal matters.

Upon arriving at the office in the morning, you check your e-mail and find the following message from Amanda Arnold, a senior partner at your law firm, who is the billing partner for the Bargain Store account:

To: You
From: Amanda Arnold <aarnold@lawfirm.com>
Subject: Bargain Store - Pls Hdl

I'm on vacation. Please respond to Jack ASAP. Send me your time sheet when you are done.
— Amanda

Begin forwarded message:

Was closing up the store at 19th and Benjamin last night and found a Rolex watch outside the building. Lea says we don't have a hard and fast rule on lost things found by employees, but she thinks we should hold it in case it belongs to a customer. I say "finders, keepers." Lea said to ask you - can I keep it?
— Jack

The Location of the Found Watch

Bargain Store

You call Jack and have a 15-minute conversation. During this conversation you learn that the found watch is shiny and in new condition. Jack found the watch on a three-foot-high wall located outside the back door to the store. The back door to the store leads to the customer parking lot behind the store, as shown in the accompanying diagram at left.

Based on these facts, prepare a brief e-mail response (no more than 150 words) to Jack and a time sheet entry using the forms reproduced at the end of Chapter One. The billing number for the Bargain Store is #5920AA. Your firm requires that time must be billed in ten-minute increments (e.g., 10 minutes, 20 minutes, etc.). You must submit a time entry for internal accounting purposes even though the client is billed based on a monthly retainer arrangement.

Points to Consider

1. What are the common law rules governing lost and found property? Should the watch be characterized as "lost" or merely "mislaid" property? Does the characterization matter in this situation?

2. How formal or informal should the tone be in your e-mail reply to Jack?

3. Should you record all of your time spent on this matter, including the 15 minute conversation with Jack?

Name:

E-Mail Reply

To: Jack Riley <jack@bargainstore.com>

CC:

Subject:

Dear Jack,

Sincerely,

Time Sheet Entry

Attorney Name:

Client: Billing No.:

DATE	DESCRIPTION	TIME

CHAPTER TWO

Trespass and Adverse Possession
The Misplaced Mechanical System

MONARCH MANUFACTURING COMPANY (Monarch) is a new client of your law firm. The owner of Monarch is Miranda Mesa, who is the company's president. Miranda has come to you because a problem has arisen in connection with an industrial manufacturing building owned by Monarch.

In your initial client interview with Miranda, you learned that Monarch is a manufacturing company with 500 employees. Monarch produces and services wind-powered turbines that generate electricity. Three months ago, the company signed long-term contracts to supply and service wind-powered turbines to several new utility company customers. To fulfill the terms of these contracts, Monarch needed to expand its production capacity.

Six weeks ago, Monarch purchased a 15,000-square-foot industrial building from Idelwood Furniture. Miranda relied upon her brother-in-law, a commercial real estate agent, to represent the company in the acquisition of the building. Monarch paid cash for the building and did not purchase title insurance.

The building sits on a 25,000-square-foot lot. Monarch planned to expand the existing structure by adding a 7,500-square-foot addition that would serve as the company's local office to service its new customers in the region. Last week, Miranda saw the building for the first time when she met with Hal Harley, the owner of Harley Construction. Miranda and Hal toured the facility and discussed the proposed construction of the new office and warehouse addition.

As they were walking around the outside of the building, Hal observed that the back corner of the lot was overgrown with weeds and small shrubs. Hal told Miranda that this area would have to be cleared to accommodate the new construction. As they walked through the area, Hal noticed that the mechanical system that provided heating, ventilation and air conditioning to a different industrial building located on the adjacent lot encroached upon the Monarch lot. Hal told Miranda that the HVAC system would have to be relocated to accommodate the new addition to the Monarch building.

The HVAC system sits on a concrete pad that occupies a total of 100 square feet. As vacant land, the site where the Monarch building is located is valued at $3.50 per square foot.

After her discussion with Hal, Miranda met with the owner of the adjacent property, Danielle Davis. Miranda and Danielle had the following conversation:

> *Miranda:* I need you to relocate your mechanical system immediately. The HVAC system is on my lot and I need it removed to expand the building.
>
> *Danielle:* The contractor who installed the HVAC system misplaced it. It's sat there for ten years and Idelwood never complained.
>
> *Miranda:* I don't care about Idelwood. I own the lot now and I want this junky thing moved!
>
> *Danielle:* Well, make me an offer and I'll think about it.
>
> *Miranda:* I'm not paying twice for something I already own. See you in court, sister.

Next, Miranda had the property surveyed. The survey showed that the HVAC system was located on the Monarch lot.

The Misplaced Mechanical System

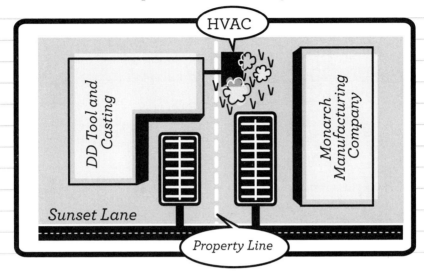

Prior to meeting with Miranda, you researched the statute of limitations governing the acquisition of title by adverse possession. State Code §15.235 provides:

> §15.235. **A person must bring suit not later than eight (8) years after the day the cause of action accrues to recover real property held in peaceable and adverse possession by another who cultivates, uses, or enjoys the property.**

Miranda has asked you to file a civil complaint against Danielle's company, DD Tool and Casting, on behalf of Monarch for trespass. You convinced Miranda that the more appropriate course of action would be to write a letter first to DD Tool and Casting demanding that the HVAC system be removed. Miranda has agreed to send a letter first, but she is unwilling to have her company pay for more than one hour of your time to write the letter.

Based on these facts, prepare a letter to Danielle Davis and DD Tool and Casting using the Demand Letter reproduced at the end of Chapter Two. Assume in writing your letter that, in addition to State Code § 15.235, the jurisdiction follows the majority common law rules in matters involving real property.

 Points to Consider

1. What are the common law elements for a trespass claim? For perfecting title to real property through adverse possession?

2. Should you anticipate and discuss a potential adverse possession defense in the demand letter?

3. Given the dollar value of the disputed real estate, does it make economic sense for the parties to take this case to trial? Will the tone of your letter make the parties more or less willing to negotiate a solution to this dispute?

Name:

Demand Letter

_____, 20____

Ms. Danielle Davis
DD Tool and Casting
634 Sunset Lane
City, State, 11123

Dear Ms. Davis,

I represent Monarch Manufacturing Company. The purpose of this letter is :

Ms Danielle Davis

Page 2

CHAPTER THREE

Gifts
The Shoe Box in the Basement

WILMA WILLOW is a long-time client of the Estate Planning Department in your law firm. Wilma's husband, Frank, is deceased. Wilma is currently 90 years old. Wilma's personal net worth is $1.5 million.[1] Much of her personal net worth is attributable to 800 shares of common stock in the South Florida State Bank (Bank). Wilma currently owns 80% of the outstanding shares of the Bank's common stock.

Last night, Wilma called and left you the following message:

> *This is Wilma Willow. I need to talk with you about giving Sam my Bank stock. I am leaving my shares to Sam in a shoe box in my basement. After I die, I want you to get the shares out of the shoe box, backdate the paperwork and then give the shares to Sam. My accountant said I needed to get the paperwork notarized. Call my accountant Cindy if you have questions. I'll see you tomorrow at noon after my morning gardening club meeting.*

After listening to Wilma's message, you pulled her client file and refreshed your memory of Wilma's situation. Your last client meeting with Wilma was eight months ago. Wilma has two adult children, her son Sam Willow and her daughter Dorothy Willow. Sam is the president of the Bank. He lives a few blocks away from Wilma and takes care of her physical needs and her finances. Dorothy is a drug addict and constantly

---

1 *You should assume for purposes of Chapter Three that Wilma's personal net worth is insufficient to raise federal estate and gift tax law issues.*

begs Wilma for money to pay her creditors. At your last client meeting with Wilma, she was worried that Dorothy's many creditors "might come after me because I have all the money." At this prior client meeting, you reviewed the terms of Wilma's Last Will and Testament (Will) with her. The Will leaves Wilma's estate in equal shares to Sam and Dorothy. You explained to Wilma that the provisions of her Will would not take effect until her death. You reassured Wilma that Dorothy's creditors would have no right to any of Wilma's property while Wilma was still alive.

The client file also contained a copy of Wilma's Bank stock certificate. The stock certificate and the form that is used to transfer ownership of the shares (known as a stock transfer power) are reproduced below. Wilma's stock transfer power is printed on the back side of her Bank stock certificate.[2]

CERTIFICATE NO. 101   **800 SHARES**

SOUTH FLORIDA STATE BANK

Incorporated Under the Laws of the State of Florida

Common Stock Par Value $1.00

This is to certify that ***Wilma Willow*** is the owner of 800 Shares of Common Stock of SOUTH FLORIDA STATE BANK, transferable on the Books of the Bank by Attorney upon the surrender of this Certificate and as provided for in the By-Laws of this Bank.

IN WITNESS WHEREOF, we have hereunto signed our names and affixed the Seal of the SOUTH FLORIDA STATE BANK at Miami, Florida.

January 1, 1952

Sara Secretary
Secretary

Frank Willow
President

---

2 *The paper Bank stock certificate and the stock transfer power reproduced above are an illustration of certificated shares. Although corporate entities may record share ownership and process the transfer of stock ownership electronically without using actual paper, many closely-held businesses still use certificated shares.*

Stock Transfer Power

FOR VALUE RECEIVED, THE UNDERSIGNED HEREBY
SELLS, ASSIGNS AND TRANSFERS UNTO

_____

_____ Shares of Common Stock of South Florida State
Bank (Bank), standing in my name on the books of the Bank,
represented by Certificate No. ___, and does hereby irrevoca-
bly constitute and appoint

_____

to transfer the Shares on the Books of the Bank.

Dated this _____ day of _____, ____.

_____.
[Signature of Transferor]

STATE OF _____

COUNTY OF _____

The foregoing instrument was acknowledged before me on

_____, _____, by _____,

[Date]   *[Year]*   *[Name of Transferor]*

an individual residing at

_____.
[Address]

_____.
[City, State]

_____.
[Signature of Notary Public]

After reviewing the client file, you called Wilma's accountant, Cindy Morales. Cindy works with a number of your estate planning clients. You had the following conversation with Cindy:

> **You:** Good morning, Cindy. I am calling you about Wilma Willow. She left a message on my office phone last night and wants to meet with me today at noon. Wilma said I could call you. Do you know what this is about?
>
> **Cindy:** Oh, yes. We met a few days ago because Wilma said she was unhappy with the county tax assessor's value for her house and she wanted to talk with me about it. After we talked about that, Wilma wanted to talk about the Bank and Sam. I think this was really what was on her mind because she had the original paper Bank stock certificate in her purse. Wilma wants to give all of her Bank stock to Sam now. She does not want Dorothy to own any part of the Bank. Wilma called Dorothy a "meth head" and said that she can't be trusted.
>
> **You:** Did you suggest that she put the gifted shares in a shoe box in her basement?
>
> **Cindy:** (Laughs) Heavens, no, I don't know anything about a shoe box in Wilma's basement. I did try to explain to her about how the shares could be transferred by filling out the stock transfer power on the back of the stock certificate. But I told her she really needed to work with you on transferring the stock to Sam. I'm not a notary public and the stock transfer power has to be dated and signed by Wilma and properly notarized to be effective.
>
> **You:** What else did you and Wilma talk about?
>
> **Cindy:** She asked a lot of questions about what would happen to the dividends from the stock once she gave the shares to Sam. Those dividends have averaged $30,000 a quarter for several years now. That's her primary income, along with Social Security.

> *You:* What did you tell her about the Bank's payment of dividends?
>
> *Cindy:* I told Wilma that once the stock transfer became effective, then the stock would be transferred to Sam on the books of the Bank and Sam would receive the dividend payments.
>
> *You:* What did Wilma think about that?
>
> *Cindy:* She didn't like that at all. She wants to keep receiving the dividends until she dies, and then let Sam have the Bank stock and the dividends. Wilma doesn't want Dorothy to own any of the Bank stock under any circumstances.
>
> *You:* Ok. Anything else I should know before I meet with Wilma? I haven't seen her in eight months.
>
> *Cindy:* I do think she has gone downhill in the last several months. She seemed confused at times about what I was telling her and didn't seem to be tracking as well as she used to.
>
> *You:* Thanks, I appreciate your help.
>
> *Cindy:* No problem. Call anytime.

It is now 11:00 a.m. and Wilma's appointment is at noon. Using the Client Counseling Outline reproduced at the end of Chapter Three, organize the key questions and discussion points you want to address in your meeting with Wilma. Can you suggest a superior arrangement to the shoe box in the basement?

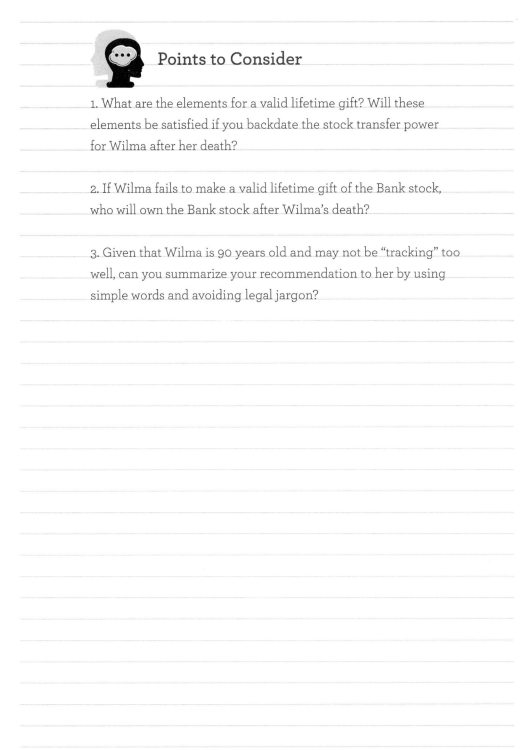

Points to Consider

1. What are the elements for a valid lifetime gift? Will these elements be satisfied if you backdate the stock transfer power for Wilma after her death?

2. If Wilma fails to make a valid lifetime gift of the Bank stock, who will own the Bank stock after Wilma's death?

3. Given that Wilma is 90 years old and may not be "tracking" too well, can you summarize your recommendation to her by using simple words and avoiding legal jargon?

Client Counseling Outline

Attorney Name:

Client:

Date:

Client Goals:

Client Concerns:

Key Questions and Discussion Points:

Recommendation

(write a summary using simple language that Wilma will understand):

CHAPTER FOUR

Present and Future Interests
No Alcohol, Smoking or Soccer Allowed

IT IS WEDNESDAY morning. You just received the following text message from Sonny Davidson, who is a client of your law firm. Sonny is a very successful local real estate developer and the president of Seaside Developers, Inc.

> Giving land to the public schools but want restrictions. Call ASAP. —Sonny

You immediately called Sonny and had the following conversation with him:

You: Hello, Sonny. I have a few minutes to talk. Your message indicated that you are giving some land to the Seaside School District?

Sonny: You know the property off of Capital Beach Boulevard you helped me buy a few years ago? The school board president called me last week and asked if I would consider donating it to the school district. They want to build athletic fields on it. It would be called the Davidson Sports Complex. I like the idea, but there's one catch.

You: What's the catch?

Sonny: I hate soccer.

You: You hate soccer? Why?

Sonny: I always wanted to play baseball. My dad made me play soccer instead. In high school I broke my leg in a varsity soccer game. I've limped ever since.

You: Did you tell the school board president that you hate soccer?

Sonny: Yes, because she said they want to put multi-purpose athletic fields on the land, and that would include soccer.

You: What did the school board president say?

Sonny: She said they could do baseball and softball fields and football and lacrosse fields instead. No soccer fields.

You: That sounds reasonable.

Sonny: There's one other thing.

You: What's that?

Sonny: I don't want any drinking or smoking going on there.

You: I think it would be tough to play lacrosse with a beer in one hand and a cigarette in the other hand.

Sonny: True, but what about the parents? There's that convenience store nearby, too. Every time I drive by, I see empty beer bottles and cans and cigarette butts on the lot. It upsets me. If my name is on the facility, I don't want it looking trashed.

You: If you give the land to the school district, you could put restrictions on the use of the land.

Sonny: Like no drinking or smoking or playing soccer?

You: Yes, but enforcing these restrictions could be problematic. You would want the school district to have a strong incentive to enforce the restrictions.

Sonny: Like they forfeit the land back to me if there's drinking or smoking or soccer going on?

You: Exactly, but legally it is a little more complicated. You have two options for how to set this deal up.

Sonny: Great! Write it up and I'll stop by tomorrow at 3:00 p.m. to sign everything.

You: Wait, Sonny! I need to explain your choices to you and you have to make a decision.

Sonny: They're calling my group to tee off. I have to turn off my cell phone. Write me an executive summary and e-mail it to my office. I'll read it tonight and make a decision. Have all the paperwork ready for either option. I'll sign one and this deal is done. See you tomorrow afternoon!

99

You worked with a senior partner in your law firm, Alicia McDoland, when Seaside Developers originally acquired the Capital Beach Boulevard property. Your firm has all client files stored electronically. After your conversation with Sonny, you located the .pdf file with the documentation from the closing on the Capital Beach Boulevard property. The deed by which Seaside Developers acquired title to the real estate is reproduced on the following page.

Warranty Deed

Larry and Laura Tribble, husband and wife ("GRANTORS"), in consideration of one dollar and other valuable consideration received from Seaside Developers, Inc., a Bliss Corporation ("GRANTEE"), hereby grant, transfer, assign and convey to GRANTEE the following described real estate:

Lots 2, 3, 4, and 5, Capital Beach Boulevard Development, City of Seaside, County of Genuine, State of Bliss.

GRANTORS covenant with GRANTEE that GRANTORS:

(1) are lawfully seized of such real estate and that the real estate is free from encumbrances, except for any easements, covenants, reservations and restrictions now of record;

(2) have legal power and lawful authority to convey the same; and

(3) warrant and will defend title to the real estate against the lawful claims of all persons.

Executed on this 16th day of March, 2009.

Larry Tribble	*Laura Tribble*
Larry Tribble	Laura Tribble

STATE OF BLISS

COUNTY OF GENUINE

The foregoing instrument was acknowledged before me on March 16, 2009, by Larry Tribble and Laura Tribble, husband and wife.

Nathan Notary

Notary Public

After reviewing the deed, you walked down the hallway and told Alicia about Sonny's phone call:

> **You:** Sonny Davidson just called me.
>
> **Alicia:** Bet he was on the golf course.
>
> **You:** I talked to him just before he had to tee off. He wants to give the Capital Beach Boulevard property to the Seaside School District for athletic fields.
>
> **Alicia:** Sounds simple enough. I'm tied up with this regional retail center deal right now. You go ahead and draft the deed to the school district. Use the firm's General Warranty Deed form.
>
> **You:** Sonny wants to put some restrictions on the use of the property. No alcohol, smoking or soccer allowed.
>
> **Alicia:** No soccer – that's weird. Is the school district okay with those restrictions?
>
> **You:** Sonny said yes, but I'll confirm that. Any preference as between a fee simple determinable or a fee simple subject to condition subsequent?
>
> **Alicia:** I always prefer the fee simple subject to condition subsequent, but of course Sonny has to make the final decision. Sorry to cut you off, but I've got to catch a plane to attend a zoning board meeting on this retail center deal. Take care of Sonny. He can be a pain sometimes, but he always pays the legal bill.

Using the two General Warranty Deed forms provided at the end of Chapter Four, draft the appropriate language to convey a fee simple subject to condition subsequent and a fee simple determinable interest in the Capital Beach Boulevard property from Seaside Developers, Inc., to the Seaside School District. In drafting the conveyance language, assume that the jurisdiction generally follows the common law rules on matters of real property, with the exception of the following statutory provisions.

> **Bliss State Code §15.08**. An otherwise effective conveyance or property transfers the entire interest which the conveyor has and has the power to convey, unless an intent to transfer a lesser interest is manifested. No words of inheritance or other special words are necessary to transfer a fee simple.
>
> **Bliss State Code §15.09**. Possibilities of reverter or rights of reentry for breach of condition subsequent shall be inheritable, assignable, alienable and devisable.

After preparing the two General Warranty Deeds, prepare the executive summary that you will e-mail to Sonny using the Memorandum form reproduced at the end of Chapter Four.

 ## Points to Consider

1. What are the relative advantages and disadvantages for Seaside Developers, Inc., of conveying a fee simple subject to condition subsequent or a fee simple determinable interest in the Capital Beach Boulevard property to the Seaside School District? Can you think of some of the practical reasons why the senior partner Alicia prefers the fee simple subject to condition subsequent estate over the fee simple determinable estate?

2. What language and punctuation unambiguously will convey a fee simple determinable interest in the Capital Beach Boulevard property to the Seaside School District? A fee simple subject to condition subsequent interest?

3. How much information must be contained in the executive summary for Sonny to make an informed decision concerning the type of defeasible present interest that his company should convey to the Seaside School District?

Name:

General Warranty Deed
(Fee Simple Subject to Condition Subsequent)

𝔚𝔞𝔯𝔯𝔞𝔫𝔱𝔶 𝔇𝔢𝔢𝔡

_____

_____

_____

_____

_____

_____

_____

_____

_____

_____

_____

GRANTOR covenants with GRANTEE that GRANTOR:

(1) is lawfully seized of such real estate and that it is free from encumbrances, except for any easements, covenants, reservations and restrictions now of record;

(2) has legal power and lawful authority to convey the same;

(3) warrants and will defend title to the real estate against the lawful claims of all persons.

Executed on this _____ day of _____, 20___ .

SEASIDE DEVELOPERS, INC.

By: _____

Sonny Davidson, President

Name: _____

General Warranty Deed
(Fee Simple Determinable)

𝔚arranty 𝔇eed

_____

_____

_____

_____

_____

_____

_____

_____

_____

_____

_____

_____

GRANTOR covenants with GRANTEE that GRANTOR:

(1) is lawfully seized of such real estate and that it is free from encumbrances, except for any easements, covenants, reservations and restrictions now of record;

(2) has legal power and lawful authority to convey the same;

(3) warrants and will defend title to the real estate against the lawful claims of all persons.

Executed on this _____ day of _____, 20____ .

SEASIDE DEVELOPERS, INC.

By: _____

Sonny Davidson, President

MEMORANDUM

To: Sonny Davidson, Seaside Developers, Inc.

From:

Re: Summary of Options for Capital Beach Boulevard Property

Memorandum, continued

CHAPTER FIVE

Co-Ownership Relationships
The Surgeons and Their Spouses

SAM CHOI AND SALLY JOHNSTON are brother and sister. You first became friends with Sam and Sally at college. Although they have very different personalities, you liked both of them as individuals. Sam was an impulsive free spirit who could cram the night before an exam and ace the test. Sally was quiet and introspective. She was always organized and planned out every detail of her life.

After college, Sam and Sally attended medical school. Upon graduating from medical school, they did their residency training in the field of pediatric surgery. Sam and Sally returned home and formed their own medical practice after completing their training.

You often see Sam and his wife, Samantha Choi, at social events. On Sunday night, you ran into Sam at a dinner and auction for a local charity and had the following conversation:

> *You:* Hi, Sam. How are things with you?
>
> *Sam:* You are just the person I wanted to see. My realtor told me I need to talk to a lawyer.
>
> *You:* You don't do house calls and I charge by the hour.
>
> *Sam:* But this is merely a social conversation between two old friends, so it's free, right?

You: I am curious, so it's free. Tell me, why does your realtor think you need a lawyer? Most realtors think they *are* lawyers.

Sam: Sally and I are buying a property that will generate rental income. Most surgeons burn out in their fifties and we want to invest for the future. An office condominium unit became available in the office park where we have our practice. We made an offer and it was accepted.

You: Do you have a tenant?

Sam: Not yet, but we don't think it will be a problem to rent it. I have a friend who is a solo orthopedic surgeon. The place is the right size and the rent is the right price for his practice. Our office park is very close to the hospital, so it is an ideal location for surgeons.

You: When do you close?

Sam: In ten days. That leads to my question. When the realtor asked how Sally and I wanted to title the property on the deed, I told her I had no idea. It's complicated because even with malpractice insurance Sally and I could take a big hit personally with a lawsuit. We thought our spouses should own the property. That's when the realtor said we needed to talk to a lawyer and get legal advice.

You: I'm always happy to have new clients. Could all of you stop by my office together later this week?

Sam: Later this week is perfect. I'll talk to Sally and we'll make an appointment with our spouses. I'll text you the contact information for my realtor and she can fill you in on the details of the deal.

"

Sally called your secretary on Monday morning and made an appointment on Thursday at 1:00 p.m. for the group. Samantha and Sally's husband, Steve Johnston, will attend this meeting along with Sam and Sally. You have never met Sally's husband, Steve, before.

On Monday afternoon, you contacted Sam's realtor, who provided the following additional information. The property is Condominium Unit #3 in the Mountain View Office Park. The seller is Medcollect, LLC, a company that provides billing and collection services for health care professionals. The office park was developed five years ago. All of the units were sold within three months after the construction was completed. A diagram of the office park, including Unit #3, is reproduced below.

Mountain View Office Park

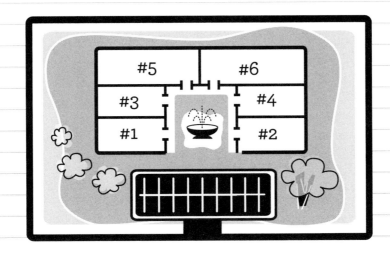

Unit #3 contains 2,200 square feet. The purchase price for the unit is $150 per square foot, which will be paid in cash. The Chois and the Johnstons will each pay one-half of the purchase price. The rental income for units in the office park averages $15.50 per square foot net of expenses. Unit #3 was on the market for only two days. After the seller signed the sales contract and the property was withdrawn from the market, the seller received two additional offers to purchase Unit #3.

It is now 11:00 a.m. on Thursday morning. Using the New Client Information Form reproduced at the end of Chapter Five, prepare an outline of the questions and discussion points you want to address during your initial client interview with the Chois and the Johnstons.

Points to Consider

1. What form of co-ownership will you recommend to your new clients? Why? Would your legal advice change if Unit #3 is located in a community property jurisdiction? (Note: If you would like to try drafting the conveyance language creating the co-ownership relationship, use the General Warranty Deed form that is reproduced at the end of Chapter Five.)

2. Given the distinctly different personalities of Sam and Sally, how likely is it that the Chois and the Johnstons always will agree on how to manage their rental property? Absent a written operating agreement for the management of the property, what are the rules that will determine the rights and duties of these co-owners?

3. As new clients, what other topics will you want to address with the Chois and the Johnstons as part of the initial client interview?

New Client Information Form

Attorney:

Client Name(s):

Billing Address:

Preferred Phone Number:

E-Mail Address:

Date of Initial Meeting:

Purpose of Initial Meeting:

Client Objective(s):

Discussion Points:

Engagement Letter Status

___ Client Declined Engagement

___ Attorney Refused Engagement

___ Engagement Letter Submitted to Client

___ Engagement Letter Returned and Filed

General Warranty Deed

MEDCOLLECT, LLC ("GRANTOR"), grants, transfers, assigns and conveys Condominium Unit #3, Mountain View Office Park, City of Mountain View, State of Paradise, to SAMANTHA CHOI and STEVE JOHNSTON and their heirs (collectively, "GRANTEES"),

_____

_____

_____

_____

_____

_____

GRANTOR covenants with GRANTEES that GRANTOR:

    (1) is lawfully seized of such real estate and that it is free from encumbrances, except for any easements, covenants, reservations and restrictions now of record;

    (2) has legal power and lawful authority to convey the same; and

    (3) warrants and will defend title to the real estate against the lawful claims of all persons.

Executed on this _____ day of _____, 20___ .

MEDCOLLECT, LLC

_____

By: Marvin Albright, President

CHAPTER SIX

Landlord and Tenant Relationships
Pets Galore

HENRY HERNANDEZ IS A REAL ESTATE DEVELOPER who specializes in building commercial and retail properties and leasing them to local businesses. Hernandez recently completed the construction of a 10,000-square-foot office warehouse building. A diagram of the building is reproduced below.

The Hernandez Building

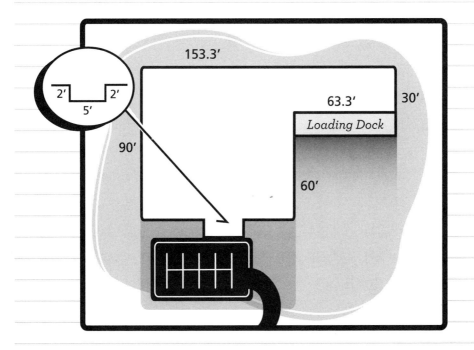

The interior of the building is unfinished shell space.[1] Hernandez wants to lease the building before finishing the shell space so that the interior layout can be customized to suit the needs of the tenant's business. The building has a small parking lot with sufficient parking for only eight vehicles. Additional tenant parking is available one block away at a neighborhood retail center owned by Hernandez.

In your local real estate market, the typical office warehouse building consists of 7% finished interior office space and 93% warehouse space. Annual rents for newly constructed office warehouse space range from $4.50 to $6.00 per square foot. Due to higher than normal vacancy rates for commercial properties in recent months, property owners are offering rent concessions to new business tenants. Rent concessions range from one to four months of free rent at the commencement of the lease.

For new construction, lease terms range from three to five years. The duration of the lease term depends on multiple factors, but the most important factor is the cost that the landlord or the tenant pays at the commencement of the lease to finish out the interior shell space. As a general rule of thumb, the larger the sum a party pays for customized interior finish, the longer that party will want the lease to be.

For office warehouse space, the tenant usually pays for all utilities and the cost to repair normal wear and tear of the premises. The tenant also usually pays for the maintenance of the building's interior and mechanical systems, such as the heating, cooling and plumbing systems. The tenant or the landlord may pay for mowing, landscaping and snow removal from the parking lot during the winter months. The landlord usually pays for the exterior maintenance of the building's walls and roof. The landlord also usually pays for the real estate taxes on the property and for casualty insurance.

---

1 *Unfinished shell space means that the property has a dirt or gravel floor, bare partitioning, and rough retail-grade electrical and plumbing systems installed, but no heating or cooling units.*

Pet Lovers Products (PLP) is an Internet-based business that specializes in unique items for pets. PLP's business is compatible with the zoning for the site where Hernandez's office warehouse building is located. Brenda Bordeau, the president of PLP, originally started the business in 2002. In 2008, Bordeau became a quadriplegic as a result of a snow boarding accident. Bordeau's employees operated the business until she recovered from her injuries. In 2010, Bordeau acquired a trained capuchin monkey named Sammy to assist her in her daily tasks. Sammy serves as Bordeau's "hands" by doing manual tasks for her, particularly tasks involving the computer and the telephone.

After Bordeau acquired Sammy, she adopted a company policy that all employees are permitted to bring their pets with them to work each day. In addition, on the first Friday of every month the employees and their pets sample the prospective new merchandise that the company is evaluating.

Today, PLP has annual gross revenues of $2,000,000. PLP purchases most of its inventory from small vendors. The products are shipped to the warehouse of PLP. Upon arrival at the warehouse, the staff updates the Internet inventory list of the company's products. Most orders are taken over the Internet and shipped directly to customers. PLP uses United Parcel Service for all of its customer shipping. The business has three full-time customer service representatives on-site to answer telephone and e-mail inquiries from its customers. PLP has a total of ten employees who work at the business during the week. The company also employs part-time workers on the weekends to stock and catalog its inventory.

You have been assigned to represent either Hernandez or PLP as your client. Your task is to negotiate the terms of a lease between

Hernandez and PLP for the office warehouse building. Your negotiation session should last for a maximum period of 50 minutes. Prior to conducting the negotiation, you met privately with your client and acquired additional information about the client's goals and objectives in leasing the office warehouse building.

In conducting your negotiation, use the Checklist of Lease Terms reproduced at the end of Chapter Six as a guide. Record the points of agreement by the parties on the Checklist. Before beginning your negotiation session, review the supplemental material on Negotiation Theory and Negotiation Lines and Phrases that follows the Checklist of Lease Terms.

 Points to Consider

1. What is your client's primary objective in negotiating the terms of the lease? What particular features or terms of the lease are the most important to your client? The least important?

2. As you negotiate, can you discern the other side's most important objective? Is this objective contrary to your client's goal, or can a win-win compromise be reached through negotiation?

3. If the other party demands that you explain or justify your client's position, to what extent may you reveal information acquired during your private client interview during the negotiation process?

Negotiator(s) for Landlord:

Negotiator(s) for Tenant:

Checklist of Lease Terms

Rent:

Damages Deposit:

Term of Lease:

Interior Shell Space Finish:

Total square feet of office finish:

Landlord will contribute $ per square foot for office finish

Contractor will be selected by:

Utilities:

Maintenance (interior):

Maintenance (exterior):

Maintenance (grounds and parking lot):

Parking:

Assignment and Sublease Rights of Tenant:

Rights and Duties in the Event of Catastrophic Damage to Premises:

Other Landlord Lease Covenants:

Other Tenant Lease Covenants:

Explanatory Notes (optional):

> SUPPLEMENTAL: **Negotiation Theory**

There are two primary types of bargaining. In positional bargaining, the parties view the negotiation as a zero sum game where one party's gain is equivalent to the other party's loss. In interest-based bargaining, the parties view the negotiation as a problem-solving process rather than a zero sum game. The parties are perceived to have complementary or mutual interests, so that bargaining may result in overall gains for both sides.

In positional bargaining, each party typically starts the negotiation from an extreme position (high or low rent, for example). The parties expect that small concessions gradually will be made by each side until a moderate or middle ground outcome is reached. Bluffing and puffing is common as the parties negotiate. When an attorney negotiates on behalf of a client, however, lying is prohibited as a violation of the lawyer's professional responsibilities under Rule 4.1 of the *Model Rules of Professional Conduct*.

Common strategies used in positional bargaining are:
(1) make the other side offer first;
(2) make the other side compromise first;
(3) claim a lack of authority to do what the other side requests;
(4) act irrationally; and
(5) claim that the other side is irrational or making unreasonable demands.

In interest-based bargaining, each party focuses on the problem to be solved and tries to identify at least one area of common interest where mutual gains may be achieved. Creative solutions are used to accommodate the goals and objectives of the parties.

Common strategies used in interest-based bargaining are:
(1) focus on the problem, not the people or their personalities;
(2) focus on the mutual interests of the parties, not on fixed demands or positions;
(3) emphasize points of collaboration, not confrontation; and
(4) empathize with the needs of the other side.

Depending on the circumstances, lawyers who are effective negotiators often use a combination of positional and interest-based bargaining to achieve the best result for their clients.

> SUPPLEMENTAL: **Negotiation Lines and Phrases**

If you enjoy playing poker, you are likely to enjoy negotiating. The list of negotiation lines and phrases below will give you a sense of how to play the negotiation game.

Tenant

1. The rent you are demanding is for a property that is perfect. This property is not perfect. [Describe deficiencies or defects in the property.]

2. Your allowance for interior finish is inadequate. If my client has to supplement the allowance, then we want a corresponding reduction in the rent.

3. If my client is contributing to the cost of the interior finish, then my client wants to pick the contractor to do the work.

4. The [insert characteristic, e.g., parking, loading dock, etc.] for this property is inadequate when compared with similar properties for rent in this market. That calls for a rent reduction.

5. There is a surplus of vacant office warehouse space in the market right now. Can't you be more reasonable?

6. Other landlords would love to work with my client. Why can't you be more accommodating?

7. Is your client prejudiced against my client because my client is [insert client characteristic]?

Landlord

1. This is quality new construction with a generous allowance for standard interior finish. My client has to cover the costs and expenses of construction and still meet payroll.

2. If my client has to pay extra for the interior finish, then the rent will go up.

3. My client needs to select the contractor to ensure quality control over the work product.

4. Vacancy rates are higher for older buildings; this is new construction.

5. Lots of tenants would love the deal I am offering.

6. My client has been in the business of owning and operating investment real estate for many years. This is a reasonable offer.

7. It is not reasonable for your tenant to demand that my client must pour more money into this asset.

8. Can you really afford to lease this property?

Generic (Anyone)

1. Do you really think that is a potential problem? Why are you so worried about something that is so unlikely to happen?

2. My client will never agree to that term.

3. I'll try to reason with my client, but you shouldn't expect too much.

4. No one can predict the future. My client needs flexibility.

5. I understand your client needs flexibility. But my client needs flexibility, too.

6. Your client would have to agree and sign off on that provision.

7. I can't advise my client to sign that.

8. Everyone has to give up something to make this deal happen.

9. Is that your best offer?

10. I've talked with my client, and this is my best offer.

11. My client is honest and has integrity. My client would never do such a bad thing.

12. This is how everyone else in town does it.

13. We need to address this issue expressly in the lease. I don't want to end up litigating over it.

CHAPTER SEVEN

Real Estate Disclosures
The Money Pit

VIRGINIA VALENTINA BECAME your client when she discovered that her "dream home" is actually a money pit. You agreed to represent Virginia in litigation on a contingency fee basis. Last week you filed a civil complaint on her behalf in state district court.

Your client first contacted you three months ago. She was upset because she had just discovered that her new home was infested with active termites. During your initial interview with Virginia, you learned the following background information.

Virginia is employed as a manager in the Department of Health and Human Services for the state government. She is single and had always wanted to own her own home. With an outstanding student loan debt of over $100,000, however, she thought home ownership was not in her future.

Over her lunch break, Virginia enjoyed taking walks through the older neighborhood near the downtown state office building where she worked. The neighborhood was first developed in the 1920s with narrow two-story row houses made of brick and stone. Due to its close proximity to downtown, the row houses attracted professionals who were interested in an urban lifestyle. Virginia occasionally pulled the real estate listing sheets out of the boxes attached to the "for sale" signs in the neighborhood. Although Virginia loved the neighborhood, the prices for the row houses were far beyond what she thought she would ever be able to afford.

Real estate prices in the neighborhood skyrocketed for several years. An economic recession then caused the market bubble to burst. The price of homes in the neighborhood fell sharply as the state government, which was the largest employer in the downtown area, laid off workers due to budgetary restrictions. Virginia continued to watch the real estate activity in the neighborhood during her noontime walks. On a whim, she even made a lowball offer on one home that was in foreclosure proceedings. The offer was refused because it was less than the mortgage held by the foreclosing bank.

Six months ago, Virginia's grandfather died, leaving her as the beneficiary of a life insurance policy worth $1 million. Virginia immediately paid off her student loan debt and began to think about buying a home in her favorite neighborhood. Her friends cautioned her that real estate was a "bad" investment. Virginia decided that if she purchased a home, she would pay for it with the cash remaining from her inheritance rather than laboring under a high monthly mortgage payment. She also vowed not to be a naive first-time home buyer. She would bargain hard and not overpay for her first home.

One day, Virginia noticed a sign outside one of the row houses. Virginia sent a message expressing interest in the home. The owner, Phillip Shively, replied and asked her to meet him at a nearby coffee shop to talk. Shively told Virginia that he was a bachelor who worked during the day as a computer programmer. His uncle was in the construction business. Shively had spent his summers during college building houses for his uncle's construction company.

Shively told Virginia he had purchased the row house three years ago with the intention of renovating it and keeping it for himself. Shively lost his job six months after purchasing the row house. While Shively was unemployed, he finished the renovations on the house. Shively told

Virginia that he recently had obtained a new job in another city. Shively needed to sell the row house quickly in order to purchase a house near his new job. Shively told Virginia that four other individuals had contacted him about the row house and were interested in looking at it.

Virginia told Shively that she was a cash buyer and she could close immediately. Shively then invited Virginia to tour the renovated row house. Virginia thought that the row house had been beautifully redone. In particular, the basement area had been completely renovated with new walls, a new ceiling with new lighting, and new carpet. The basement was light and airy and just perfect for entertaining guests.

Moving cautiously before making an offer, Virginia hired a real estate appraiser to provide her with market data concerning the value of the house. Virginia did not personally know any home inspectors. Her sister-in-law recommended a friend, who had just completed his training and had been hired as an inspector at a well-established home inspection company. The company was a reputable one, and so Virginia hired the friend to do the home inspection.

Virginia toured the home with the home inspector. Shively also attended the home inspection. The inspector had several questions about the basement renovation work. Shively answered these questions to the satisfaction of the inspector. Based on the market data and the results of the home inspection, Virginia made an all-cash offer for $450,000 for the row house. Shively immediately accepted the offer. The transaction closed two weeks later and Virginia moved into the row house. Shively did not leave Virginia a forwarding address.

About three and a half months ago, Virginia was cleaning up the basement after hosting a party for several of her friends. She noticed some black specks along the baseboard of the wall. Virginia swept up the specks, but she wondered about them. Several days later, the specks reappeared. She also noticed a small black bug on the wall. The bug

• LITIGATING DISCLOSURE CLAIMS

scampered behind the electrical outlet cover before she could catch it.

Terrified that her messy friends (combined with her less-than-diligent housekeeping) might have triggered a cockroach infestation in the basement, Virginia called the first pest control company listed in the telephone directory, A-1 Pest Control. The person who answered Virginia's call told her not to disturb any signs of insects and that a technician would meet her to inspect the home on Friday after work.

Virginia watched the black specks along the baseboard build up as she waited for Friday. When the A-1 technician arrived on Friday, she took him down to the basement and showed him the black specks that had accumulated along the baseboard. The technician immediately called the owner of the company, Brad, who had operated the business for over 25 years. Together, the technician and the owner examined the basement without saying a word to Virginia.

At the conclusion of the inspection, Brad told Virginia that he was "90% certain" that there were active termites behind the newly refinished basement walls. Brad asked Virginia if he could cut a small hole in the Sheetrock of the basement wall and insert a microscopic camera to see behind the wall. Stunned, Virginia agreed. The camera showed a large number of active termites at work munching on the wooden beams that supported the first floor of the row house. The camera also showed that several of the older beams had been literally eaten away, and that temporary support beams had been installed to prop up the first floor structure. After Brad showed the termite damage to Virginia, she contacted you to represent her in litigation against the seller Phillip Shively.

*Sorry, Lady! I'm **90%** certain...*

Since your initial client meeting with Virginia, you hired a private investigator, who located Phillip Shively and provided you with Shively's residential address for service of process. You hired Brad to prepare an estimate of the cost to treat the home for termites. You hired a retired general contractor with over 40 years in the residential construction business to examine the structural damage from the termites. The contractor discovered that much of the electrical wiring, which was revealed once the Sheetrock was removed in the basement, was improperly installed. The total estimated cost to treat the termites, repair the structural termite damage, correctly install the electrical wiring and restore the basement to its prior condition is $175,000.

Virginia also provided you with the seller information form that Shively gave to her during their initial meeting at the coffee house. The Seller Property Condition Disclosure Statement form was signed by Shively. In reviewing the disclosure statement, you noticed the following relevant provisions:

Seller Property Condition Disclosure Statement

THIS STATEMENT IS A DISCLOSURE OF THE CONDITION OF THE REAL PROPERTY KNOWN BY THE SELLER ON THE DATE ON WHICH THIS STATEMENT IS SIGNED. THE INFORMATION PROVIDED IN THIS STATEMENT IS THE REPRESENTATION OF THE SELLER WITH REGARD TO THE PHYSICAL CONDITION OF THE SELLER'S REAL PROPERTY.

Section B. Electrical Systems

Have you ever experienced any problems with the electrical system or its components?

___X___ No   ____Yes

Section E. Structures

Has there been any damage to the real property or any of the structures thereon due to the following occurrences including, but not limited to, wind, hail, fire, flood, wood-destroying insects, or rodents?

___ Yes   _X_ No   ___ Do Not Know

Are there any structural problems with the structures on the real property?

___ Yes   _X_ No   ___ Do Not Know

Virginia told you that when her neighbor noticed the A-1 Pest Control van parked in front of the row house, the neighbor came over to talk with her. The neighbor told Virginia that while Shively was renovating the property, a Z-Best Pest Control van was parked in front of the row house for several days. The neighbor remembered the name on the van because the neighbor later hired Z-Best Pest Control to spray for silverfish that had infested the attic of his house. The neighbor told Virginia that he thought Z-Best Pest Control was "terrible" and wanted to know how she liked the service from A-1 Pest Control.

Based on this information, you prepared and filed a civil complaint against Shively on behalf of Virginia. The complaint contained two counts. Count One was a claim for fraudulent misrepresentation based on Shively's written representations in the Seller Property Condition Disclosure Statement. Count Two was a claim for breach of the seller's duty to disclose latent defects in the physical condition of the property that are known to the seller and not discoverable by the buyer upon a reasonable inspection. (Assume that your jurisdiction imposes this affirmative duty to disclose latent defects upon the seller.)

Shively's attorney has moved to dismiss Virginia's complaint for failure to state a claim for which relief can be granted. The standard of judicial review for a motion to dismiss in your jurisdiction is identical to the standard under Federal Rule of Civil Procedure 12(b)(6). Regarding Count One, Shively denied making any statements to Virginia regarding the physical condition of the row house. Regarding Count Two, Shively admitted he did do the renovation work on the house, but denied having knowledge of any defects in the physical condition of the row house.

You now must respond in writing to Shively's motion to dismiss. Refer to the Plaintiff's Brief in Opposition to Defendant's Motion to Dismiss, which is reproduced at the end of Chapter Seven. Begin by writing the introduction section of the Plaintiff's Brief. The introduction section should provide the court with the background of the case and summarize the alleged facts that support the two claims asserted in Virginia's complaint.

After writing the introduction section, prepare an outline for the argument section of the Plaintiff's Brief. Your outline should contain two main sections that correspond to the two counts in Virginia's complaint. For each count of the complaint, draft a main heading followed by several subheadings. In outlining your argument, write only the brief's major headings and subheadings. Do not attempt to write the body of the brief. Assume that under your court's local procedural rules, the entire brief must be limited to no more than 15 pages once it is written. Therefore, it is important to begin by making the main headline and subheadings of the Plaintiff's Brief as concise and persuasive as possible.

Points to Consider

1. What elements must Virginia allege to survive a motion to dismiss for each claim? (These elements will determine the relevant factual information that should be included in the introduction section of your brief.)

2. What facts support the elements of Virginia's fraudulent misrepresentation claim? Her failure to disclose claim? Can some facts be used to support both claims? Can you use common facts to consolidate certain points in the outline of your argument?

3. How will the tone of the language you use in the main headings and subheadings of your brief affect the persuasive power of your arguments?

Name:

Plaintiff's Brief in Opposition
to Defendant's Motion to Dismiss

IN THE STATE DISTRICT COURT

VIRGINIA VALENTINA,	)	
	)	
Plaintiff,	)	Case No. Civ-04B-285
	)	
v.		
	)	
PHILLIP SHIVELY,	)	
	)	Jury Trial Demanded
Defendant	)	

PLAINTIFF'S BRIEF IN OPPOSITION TO
DEFENDANT'S MOTION TO DISMISS

Pursuant to State Rule of Civil Procedure 12(b)(6), Plaintiff submits the following brief in opposition to Defendant's motion to dismiss Plaintiff's claims.

I. Introduction

II. Affirmative Misrepresentation Claim

Main Heading:

Subheadings:

III. Failure to Disclose Claim

Main Heading:

Subheadings:

Conveying Title to Real Estate
For Sale: Memorial Stadium

TITLE TO REAL PROPERTY is transferred when the grantor delivers a written deed to the grantee that satisfies the requirements of the Statute of Frauds. To satisfy the common law version of the Statute of Frauds, the deed must: (1) identify the grantor and the grantee; (2) provide a legal description of the real estate conveyed; (3) contain words of conveyance; and (4) be signed by the party to be bound (the grantor).[1]

Using these elements and the Quit Claim Deed reproduced at the end of Chapter Eight, prepare a deed purporting to convey title to your favorite collegiate or professional football stadium to your professor. (If you do not have a favorite stadium, "Memorial Stadium" will suffice.) You will be the grantor and your professor will be the grantee on this deed. For the legal description of the real estate, you may assume that an attached "Appendix A" to the deed contains a full legal description. Pause now and allow yourself no more than ten minutes to prepare the Quit Claim Deed.

The Quit Claim Deed you prepared should contain no promises ("covenants") concerning the validity of the legal title conveyed by the deed. As a result, neither your professor, nor anyone else that your professor subsequently might convey title to, can bring a claim against you based on your Quit Claim Deed.

---

1 *Some states by statute impose additional requirements for a valid deed. For purposes of the drafting exercises in Chapter Eight, you should assume that the jurisdiction applies the common law version of the Statute of Frauds.*

Although a quit claim deed is sufficient to convey legal title to real estate, in practice real estate attorneys usually draft deeds that contain more information than simply the bare minimum elements necessary to satisfy the Statute of Frauds. The Deed Drafting Checklist below summarizes the features or elements that typically are incorporated into real estate deeds.

Deed Drafting Checklist

- ❑ *Names of grantor and grantee*
- ❑ *Words of conveyance*
- ❑ *Legal description of the property conveyed*
- ❑ *Signature of the grantor*
- ❑ *Date of conveyance*
- ❑ *Consideration paid*
- ❑ *Deed covenants*
- ❑ *Encumbrances that are exceptions to the deed's covenants*
- ❑ *Notarization of grantor's signature*

The date of conveyance is used to document priority for purposes of the jurisdiction's recording act statute. If the conveyance is a purchase and sale transaction, the deed will indicate that consideration has been paid so that the grantee may claim bona fide purchaser status in the event of a title dispute. Usually, the purchase price itself is not contained in the deed. Instead, real estate lawyers indicate that the deed is given in exchange for a dollar amount ($1.00 or $10.00 or $100.00) and "other good and valuable consideration."

In an arm's length sale transaction, usually the buyer insists that the deed must contain covenants regarding the quality of the legal title to the real estate. The three standard present deed covenants are the covenant of seisin, the covenant of the right to convey, and the covenant against encumbrances. The three standard future deed covenants are for quiet enjoyment, warranty and further assurances.[2]

Deed covenants present drafting choices for the grantor's attorney, who typically prepares the deed in a sale transaction. The deed language may include exceptions for certain encumbrances on the property.[3] For example, assume that the deed contains a covenant against encumbrances that is "subject to all encumbrances of record." This language effectively incorporates by reference the jurisdiction's real estate recording system into the provisions of the deed and requires the grantee to accept any recorded encumbrances. The grantee who accepted such a deed would not waive the right to sue the grantor for a title defect related to an unrecorded encumbrance, such as a prescriptive or implied easement right.

Compare the above language with a deed covenant declaring that "the real estate is free of all encumbrances, subject to all easements, covenants and private restrictions." By accepting a deed with this covenant language, the grantee accepts all title defects related to *both* recorded *and* unrecorded encumbrances on the real estate.

A third drafting option (and one preferred by many sophisticated buyers of real estate) is to list precisely the specific encumbrances that are exceptions to the deed's covenant against encumbrances. This approach avoids incorporating the jurisdiction's recording system (with all of its flaws) into the deed as a blanket waiver of recorded encumbrances on the property.

---

2 *In some states, by state statute these covenants are incorporated by reference and need not be stated expressly in the deed.*

3 *Examples of encumbrances include easement rights, restrictive covenants and mortgage interests.*

For the attorney who prepares the deed, other drafting choices involve how far back in time the covenants in the deed are to extend. If the grantor delivers a special warranty deed, the grantor can only be sued if the title defect that resulted in a breach of a deed covenant arose while the grantor owned the property. A special warranty deed precludes the grantor from suing for a breach of one of the covenants in the deed for any title defect that arose before the grantor owned the property.[4] If the grantor delivers a general warranty deed, the grantor can be sued for breach of the deed's covenants for any title defect that arose before or during the time the grantor owned the property (even if the grantor is ignorant of the title defect).

From a negotiation perspective, the grantor generally prefers to deliver a special warranty deed. The grantee generally prefers to accept a general warranty deed. In a sale transaction, the type of deed to be delivered by the seller to the buyer at the closing should be specified in the real estate sales contract.

It is not uncommon for the heading at the top of the deed instrument to state simply that the instrument is a "Warranty Deed" without identifying the types or duration of the covenants made by the grantor. The covenant language that creates a special warranty deed is fairly cryptic. Note that the covenant language in the illustration of a special warranty deed is in bold type on the following page. It is these few additional bolded words that create a special warranty deed. To create a general warranty deed, these bolded words are omitted.

---

4 *Obviously, no grantor can be sued for title defects that arise after the grantor has conveyed away title to the property.*

Special Warranty Deed Covenants

GRANTOR covenants with GRANTEE that GRANTOR:

(1) is lawfully seized of such real estate and that it is free from encumbrances, except for any easements, covenants, reservations and restrictions now of record;

(2) has legal power and lawful authority to convey the same; and

(3) warrants and will defend title to the real estate against the lawful claims of all persons <u>claiming the same or any part thereof through, by or under Grantor.</u>

Finally, the grantor's signature on the deed is witnessed by a notary public (or notarized). Although a deed does not need to be notarized to transfer legal title to the property from the grantor to the grantee, only notarized documents and instruments may be recorded in the real estate records system.

With this background information in mind, prepare the Special Warranty Deed reproduced at the end of Chapter Eight. Your Special Warranty Deed should be no more than four pages in length.

In preparing the Special Warranty Deed, assume that the grantor is Elevation Roofing Co., Inc., a Gold State corporation (Elevation). Your client is Elevation. The grantee is Morrison General Contractors, Inc., a Silver State corporation (Morrison). Morrison is paying Elevation $575,000 in consideration for the property. The legal description for the real estate to be conveyed by Elevation is:

Lot Six, Adamson Industrial Park 3rd Addition, City of Diamond, Jewel County, Gold State.

Jewel County has a grantor-grantee index for its recording system. A title search of the real estate revealed the following encumbrances of record:

- An ingress and egress easement right granted for the benefit of Lot Seven (recorded at Book 189, Page 174);

- An electrical utility line easement for the benefit of the Diamond City Electric Company (recorded at Book 195, Page 62); and

- Water and sewer line easements for the benefit of the Jewel County Public Water Company (recorded at Book 198, Page 1003).

The Special Warranty Deed is to be delivered by the grantor Elevation tomorrow at the closing. The closing will take place at your office.

Points to Consider

1. What language will create the most favorable covenant against encumbrances from the perspective of your client, the grantor Elevation?

2. Assume that instead of representing Elevation, you represent Morrison. Would you advise your client to accept a deed with covenant language purporting to convey title to the real estate "free from all encumbrances, except for any easements, covenants, reservations and restrictions"?

3. Which officer for Elevation must execute the Special Warranty Deed so that the present deed covenant of the right to convey is not breached when the deed is delivered at the closing tomorrow morning?

Name: _____

Quit Claim Deed

𝕯𝖊𝖊𝖉

_____, an individual residing

in _____ ("GRANTOR"), in consideration

of one dollar and other valuable consideration received from

_____ ("GRANTEE"), hereby conveys to

GRANTEE the property known as:

_____ Stadium,

a legal description of which is attached hereto as Appendix A.

Executed on this _____ day of _____, 20___ .

_____

Grantor

STATE OF _____)

) ss

COUNTY OF _____)

The foregoing instrument was acknowledged before me on

_____ , 20___ , by_____ ,

a resident of   _____.

_____

Notary Public

Name:

Special Warranty Deed

𝔚arranty 𝔇eed

_____

_____

_____

_____

_____

_____

_____

_____

_____

_____

_____

_____

_____

_____

_____

_____

_____

_____

_____

_____

_____

_____

_____

_____

_____

_____

_____

_____

Special Warranty Deed, continued

_____

_____

_____

_____

_____

_____

_____

_____

_____

_____

_____

_____

_____

_____

_____

_____

_____

_____

_____

_____

_____

_____

_____

_____

_____

_____

_____

_____

_____

_____

_____

_____

_____

_____

_____

_____

_____

Special Warranty Deed, continued

_____

_____

_____

_____

_____

_____

_____

_____

_____

_____

_____

_____

_____

_____

_____

_____

_____

_____

_____

_____

_____

_____

_____

_____

_____

_____

_____

_____

_____

_____

_____

_____

_____

_____

_____

_____

Special Warranty Deed, continued

CHAPTER NINE

Easements
Seeds and Signs

BELAIRE OUTDOOR ADVERTISING, INC. (Belaire) is a local company incorporated in the State of Composure that specializes in installing and operating digital billboards. The company's main customers are national chains, such as retailers, restaurants and convenience stores, that are located off of major highways. Belaire typically acquires the easement rights for its billboards from farmers whose crop land is adjacent to the roadway.

The general counsel for Belaire is Dolores Regas. Prior to becoming general counsel at Belaire, Dolores was a partner in your firm's Intellectual Property and Technology Practice Group. Dolores joined Belaire as its general counsel three months ago.

As a new associate in the firm, you have been assigned to the Real Estate Practice Group. The head of your firm's Real Estate Practice Group is Jonathan Belise. Jonathan is your immediate supervising attorney. Jonathan and Dolores are good friends.

After your new associate training session yesterday morning, Jonathan took you out to lunch and gave you your first "real" assignment. At lunch, Jonathan provided you with the following background information.

Belaire currently is acquiring easement rights to install digital billboards along State Highway 84, which travels through a rural area. Although State Highway 84 presently is a two-lane road, plans call for it to be expanded to four lanes in the near future. Several national retailers have signed leases for stores in an outlet mall that will be built at a new interchange where State Highway 84 intersects with U.S. Interstate 99. Belaire wants to acquire several billboard locations now before the road expansion and related retail construction increase the price to acquire the easement rights.

Belaire uses a standardized form to acquire its easement rights. This standardized form, entitled the Belaire Easement Agreement, was written over ten years ago by Belaire's former general counsel. The Belaire Easement Agreement is reproduced at the end of Chapter Nine. According to Jonathan, "Dolores was appalled at this form." Dolores has engaged Jonathan to draft a revised version of the Belaire Easement Agreement for the company to use in acquiring future billboard easement rights. Jonathan "would love to have Belaire as a client" and wants to maintain a good relationship with Dolores. Unfortunately, at the present time Jonathan is preoccupied with a $20 million real estate loan syndication deal for another client.

Your assignment from Jonathan is to examine the Belaire Easement Agreement and determine which provisions are inadequate or could be improved. To assist you in this task, Jonathan has provided you with his personal "checklist" that he uses when drafting easement agreements. Jonathan's Easement Agreement Checklist summarizes the elements and features that typically are incorporated into easement agreements.

Jonathan's Easement Agreement Checklist

☑ *Names of grantor and grantee*

☑ *Words of conveyance granting the easement*

☑ *Date of conveyance*

☑ *Duration of easement right granted*

☐ *Identify the parcel burdened by the easement*

☑ *Identify whether easement is appurtenant or in gross*

☐ *Describe the location of the easement*

☑ *Describe the scope of the easement*

☑ *Describe any restrictions on the rights of the easement holder and indicate consideration paid for the easement right*

☐ *Describe allocation of any future condemnation award*

☑ *(Easement in Gross): Indicate whether the easement right is transferable by the party who holds the easement right*

☑ *Indicate whether the easement may be relocated and whether the consent of the owner of the burdened parcel is required*

☑ *Signature(s) as necessary to satisfy the Statute of Frauds*

☑ *Unique provisions related to the use and maintenance of the easement*

☑ *Notarization of signature(s)*

Your assignment is to draft the Revised Belaire Easement Agreement using the form reproduced at the end of Chapter Nine. Before you begin preparing your draft, review the supplemental material on Easement Basics that follows the Revised Belaire Easement Agreement form.

Points to Consider

1. What type of easement — appurtenant or in gross — will Belaire be acquiring for its digital billboards? What are the elements that must be included in the Revised Bellaire Easement Agreement to create Belaire's easement right? Are all of these elements contained in the Belaire Easement Agreement? Could these elements be expressed more clearly in the Revised Belaire Easement Agreement?

2. In addition to placing the billboard on the property, what other rights in connection with the servicing and maintenance of a digital billboard should the company acquire as part of the Revised Belaire Easement Agreement?

3. The Belaire Easement Agreement is difficult for the company to administer because the "terms and conditions" provisions are unique to each landowner. In the Revised Belaire Easement Agreement, can you create a form that standardizes at least some of these terms and conditions to reduce this administrative burden?

Name: _____

Belaire Easement Agreement

This Belaire Easement Agreement ("Agreement") is made
this _____ day of _____, 20 ____ by and between
_____ ("Grantor"),
and Belaire Outdoor Advertising, Inc., a company incorporated
in the State of Composure ("Grantee").

    The Grantor does hereby grant, sell and convey unto Grantee
an easement for the location of the outdoor advertising structure or
structures (the "Easement"), which is described in Exhibit A
of this Agreement. The property to be burdened by the Easement is
described in Exhibit B of this Agreement (the "Property").

    Grantor herein grants the Easement subject to the following
terms and conditions:

_____

_____

_____

_____

_____

_____

_____

_____

_____

_____

_____

_____

_____

_____

Grantor warrants that it is the sole record owner of the Property over which the Easement is created, that such Property is not subject to any mortgages or liens, that such Property is not encumbered by any restrictions, easements, covenants, leases or other rights that are in any way conflicting with or inconsistent with the conveyance herein made, and that Grantor has the right and authority to execute this Easement Agreement and to grant, sell and convey the real property rights set forth herein to Grantee.

Executed this _____ day of _____ , 20 _____.

_____

[Signature of Grantor]

_____

President, Belaire Outdoor Advertising, Inc.

STATE OF _____

COUNTY OF _____

On this, the _____ day of , _____, 20___ before me, the undersigned, a NOTARY PUBLIC, personally appeared _____ [Grantor], known (or satisfactorily proved) to me to be the person subscribed to this instrument and acknowledged to me that [he or she] executed the same for the purposes therein contained.

IN WITNESS WHEREOF,
I hereunto set my hand and official seal.

_____

[Signature of Notary Public]

EXHIBIT A
Legal Description of the Easement

_____
_____
_____
_____
_____
_____
_____
_____
_____
_____

EXHIBIT B
Legal Description of the Property

_____
_____
_____
_____
_____
_____
_____
_____
_____
_____
_____

Name:

Revised Belaire Easement Agreement

_____
_____
_____
_____
_____
_____
_____
_____
_____
_____
_____
_____
_____
_____
_____
_____
_____
_____
_____
_____
_____
_____
_____
_____
_____
_____
_____
_____
_____
_____
_____
_____

Revised Belaire Agreement, continued

Revised Belaire Agreement, continued

_____

_____

_____

_____

_____

_____

_____

_____

_____

_____

_____

_____

_____

_____

_____

_____

_____

_____

_____

_____

_____

_____

_____

_____

_____

_____

_____

_____

_____

_____

_____

_____

_____

_____

_____

_____

Revised Belaire Agreement, continued

> SUPPLEMENTAL: **Easement Basics**

Concepts and Vocabulary

An easement is the right to enter onto land owned by another person. An easement right involves the transfer of an interest in real property. Therefore, an easement right must be created by a writing that satisfies the Statute of Frauds.

Easements are classified as either appurtenant or in gross. An appurtenant easement exists between two parcels of land that are owned by different persons. An appurtenant easement right benefits one parcel of land (known as the dominant or benefiting parcel) and burdens the parcel of land that is subject to the easement right (known as the servient or burdened parcel). The dominant and servient parcels usually are adjacent to one another. When an appurtenant easement is created, the owner of the dominant parcel has the right to use the servient parcel according to the terms and conditions of the written agreement that created the easement right.

An easement in gross exists when only one tract of land — the servient parcel that is burdened by the easement — is involved. An easement in gross is granted to a particular person (including a corporate entity such as Belaire) rather than attaching to a particular dominant parcel of land.

The person who owns the easement in gross has the right to enter onto the burdened parcel pursuant to the terms and conditions of the written agreement that created the easement right. Under the terms of the easement agreement, the parties expressly may make the benefit of the easement in gross transferable to another person. Such transferability is essential if the easement right is closely associated with the assets of a company or a business, such as the easement in gross rights associated with utility lines, railroad lines, cell phone towers or signs and billboards.

To make the benefit of the easement in gross transferable, the parties should clearly state in the easement agreement that the right is transferable. The agreement should state that the grantor of the easement right (the owner of the servient parcel) is conveying the easement right to the grantee "and [his/her/its] heirs, successors and assigns." If these provisions are used to create the easement right, then the benefit of the easement in gross may be transferred by its owner. Moreover, the burden of the easement in gross will transfer automatically to any successor owner of the servient parcel.

Similar language is used to make an appurtenant easement "run with the land" — a phrase that means the easement right transfers — transfer automatically with the transfer of ownership of the dominant and servient parcels. To make an appurtenant easement transfer automatically with a change in land ownership, the parties should specify in their agreement that the appurtenant easement is being conveyed to the grantee "and [his/her/its] heirs, successors and assigns for the benefit of [identify dominant parcel]."

Drafting Easement Agreements

What language in an easement agreement clearly creates an appurtenant easement or an easement in gross? Consider first the language below creating an appurtenant easement right that burdens Parcel A and benefits Parcel B.

Appurtenant Easement Language

Grantor grants, transfers and conveys to Grantee and his heirs, successors and assigns an appurtenant easement for the benefit of Parcel B. Such appurtenant easement shall run with the land and benefit future owners of Parcel B and burden future owners of Parcel A.

Now compare the language below creating a transferable easement in gross right that burdens Parcel A for the benefit of Party B.

Easement In Gross Language

Grantor grants, transfers and conveys to Party B and his heirs, successors and assigns an easement in gross that shall burden Parcel A. Such easement in gross shall run with the land and burden future owners of Parcel A.

The above illustrations, together with Jonathan's Easement Agreement Checklist, provide you with enough information to begin drafting the Revised Belaire Easement Agreement.

CHAPTER TEN

Takings for Public Use
The Road Improvement Project

THE STATE DEPARTMENT OF ROADS is improving 98th Street to address increased traffic volume and related safety concerns with the roadway. Over the last five years, the daily traffic count for 98th Street has increased from approximately 2,000 vehicles to 15,000 vehicles due to residential development in the area. The number of accidents on 98th Street has increased with the traffic count due to the narrow design of the roadway, which has two lanes and only an 18-inch shoulder on both sides of the road. After the improvements are completed, the road will have four traffic lanes with an adequate shoulder for the outside lanes.

In addition to its narrow width, 98th Street is prone to flooding due to Stevens Creek. Stevens Creek runs in a north-to-south direction and bisects 98th Street, which is an east-to-west roadway. During periods of heavy rain, the culvert that carries the water from Stevens Creek underneath 98th Street is inadequate in diameter. As a result, the water from Stevens Creek pools on the north side of 98th Street and flows across the road.

Part of the 98th Street improvement project involves addressing this flooding issue. The Federal Emergency Management Agency (FEMA) is in the process of updating the Flood Insurance Rate Map for the Stevens Creek area. FEMA's updates will expand the flood plain[1] north of 98th Street along both sides of Stevens Creek. In anticipation of FEMA's

---

[1] *A flood plain is an area where water pools and collects only in times of excessive rainfall. Agricultural uses are permitted in a flood plain. Residential uses are not permitted in a flood plain unless the elevation of the land is raised above the flood stage.*

changes, a proposal is pending before the local zoning authority to change the zoning regulations so that additional land on both sides of Stevens Creek is restricted solely to agricultural uses.[2] This zoning change is pending before the local zoning authority, but the requested change has not yet been enacted. The State Department of Roads also plans to deepen the channel for the Stevens Creek floodway[3] as the stream water approaches 98th Street from the north. Finally, the culvert for the floodway that goes underneath 98th Street will be expanded in diameter so that the culvert is adequate in size to prevent pooling and related flooding of 98th Street.

The proposed zoning change will impact Tract 8. Tract 8 is a working farm with a mixture of dry crop land, irrigated crop land, and grass pastureland. Tract 8 currently is zoned for agricultural uses and small acreage home sites with a minimum lot size of 10 acres. The two diagrams that follow illustrate the impact of the widening of 98th Street and the proposed flood plain zoning change on Tract 8 before and after the road improvement project is completed.

Tract 8: Before

---

2 *Under governing State Law, a landowner is not entitled to compensation when land is rezoned so that the landowner's use of the property is more restricted under the new zoning regulation.*

3 *A floodway is an area of constantly moving water.*

Tract 8: After

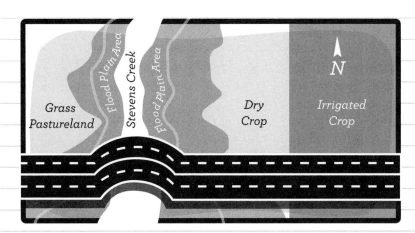

The owner of Tract 8 is Fred Farmer. A few years ago, a real estate developer approached Fred about selling the grass pastureland on the west side of Stevens Creek. In talking with the developer, Fred learned that the topography of the land to the west of Stevens Creek was ideal for the development of a residential subdivision. The developer told Fred that the grass pastureland could be subdivided into 10-acre home sites.[4] Under current zoning regulations, it is possible to develop up to six 10-acre residential lots on the grass pastureland west of Stevens Creek. After the rezoning to accommodate the expanded flood plain, it will be possible to develop only two 10-acre home sites.

The State Department of Roads engaged a private right-of-way appraisal and negotiation firm, Roadway Services, LLC (Roadway), to estimate the compensation due to Fred. Roadway estimated that the market value of Fred's dry crop land was $4,000 per acre, irrigated crop land was $5,500 per acre, and grass pastureland was $2,250 per acre. Using these market values, Roadway estimated the compensation due to Fred as follows:

---

4 *Sewer and water service cannot be extended to the east side of Stevens Creek. Residential development east of Stevens Creek is not economically feasible due to the prohibitive costs associated with drilling water wells and installing septic systems.*

Soil Type	Acres Before	Acres After	Acres Taken	Compensation
Dry Crop	160	155	5	5.0@$4,000 = **$20,000**
Irrigated Crop	80	77.5	2.5	2.5@$5,500 = **$12,500**
Grass Pastureland	80	77.5	2.5	2.5@$2,250 = **$5,625**

Total Compensation Due: $ 38,125

Based on this estimate, Roadway made an offer to Fred on behalf of the State Department of Roads. Roadway offered to pay Fred $38,125 if Fred would voluntarily transfer title to the 10 acres to the State Department of Roads.

Fred was outraged by this offer. He hired Ron Reed, MAI, SW/RA[5], to perform an appraisal of Tract 8 to determine the compensation due for the taking of his property. Ron agreed with Roadway's estimate of the total acreage that would be taken to widen 98th Street. Ron disagreed, however, with Roadway's determination that land should be valued as dry crop land, irrigated crop land and grass pastureland.

Ron determined that the highest and best use[6] of Tract 8 was not solely for agricultural purposes. Rather, Ron concluded that the highest

---

5 *An explanation of these professional credentials is contained in the Supplemental Material at the end of Chapter Ten.*

6 *The material on Highest and Best Use at the end of Chapter Ten explains how the potential use of a property impacts the determination of market value.*

and best use for the grass pastureland west of Stevens Creek was for the development of a small subdivision of country estate homes. Ron opined that the market value for residential development purposes of the grass pastureland north of 98th Street was $10,000 per acre. Based on this analysis, Ron concluded that the total compensation due to Fred for the taking of 10 acres should be $57,500, calculated as follows:

Highest Use	Acres Before	Acres After	Acres Taken	Compensation
Dry Crop	160	155	5	5.0@$4,000 = $20,000
Irrigated Crop	80	77.5	2.5	2.5@$5,500 = $12,500
Residential	*80*	*77.5*	*2.5*	*2.5@ $10,000 = $25,000*

Total Compensation Due: $57,500

Ron also told Fred that after the proposed zoning change, only two small acreage home sites could be developed on the grass pastureland to the west of Stevens Creek.

You have been assigned to represent either the State Department of Roads or Fred Farmer in negotiating the compensation due to Fred for the taking of his property. Prior to conducting the negotiation, you met privately with your client and acquired additional relevant information.

Before you formulate your negotiation strategy, review the supplemental material on Highest and Best Use and Appraisal Theory and Practice at the end of Chapter Ten. After you finish your negotiation session, prepare the Compensation Settlement Agreement at the end of Chapter Ten for your client's signature. Use the Client Memorandum that follows the Compensation Settlement Agreement to prepare a memo to your client briefly explaining the strategic factors that led to the final negotiated settlement amount.

 Points to Consider

1. Under current Supreme Court law, is Fred entitled to compensation for the potential loss of four 10-acre residential lots in the grass pastureland area west of Stevens Creek due to a change in the zoning regulations?

2. How will the prospect of litigation as an alternative solution impact your client's negotiation position?

3. Assume that if this dispute ends up in litigation, Ron Reed, MAI, SW/RA, will be an expert witness for the property owner, Fred Farmer. What information about Ron's background and qualifications would you want to acquire during discovery if you represent the State Department of Roads? If your client is the State Department of Roads, what information would you like to acquire during discovery about the business relationship between the State Department of Roads and Roadway?

Describe strengths + weaknesses

500 words, much longer than need be - less is more

Compensation Settlement Agreement

THIS COMPENSATION SETTLEMENT AGREEMENT, made on this _____ day of _____, 20_____ , by and between the STATE DEPARTMENT OF ROADS and FRED FARMER (collectively, the "Parties"), provides as follows:

WHEREAS, Fred Farmer is the owner in fee simple absolute of Tract 8, a legal description of which is set forth in Appendix A of this Agreement; and

WHEREAS, the State Department of Roads desires to acquire 10.0 acres of Tract 8 for public use, as further described in Appendix B of this Agreement (the "Property"); and

WHEREAS, the Parties have negotiated an agreement as to the amount of compensation to be paid for the Property;

NOW, THEREFORE, RESOLVED, the Parties hereby agree as follows:

1. The STATE DEPARTMENT OF ROADS shall pay FRED FARMER the sum of: _____ dollars ($_____); and

2. FRED FARMER shall execute a special warranty deed, prepared by the STATE DEPARTMENT OF ROADS, conveying fee simple absolute title to the Property to the STATE DEPARTMENT OF ROADS; and

3. FRED FARMER shall waive the right to assert all further claims and rights related to the acquisition of the Property by the STATE DEPARTMENT OF ROADS.

Agreed this _____ day of _____, 20_____ .

STATE DEPARTMENT OF ROADS

By: _____　　_____
　　　　　　　　　　　　　　　　　　　　　　　　　　FRED FARMER

-not settlement agreement. Just Client Letter   - not a lawyer
                                                  - explan all core

Client Memorandum

To:

From:

Date:

Re: Compensation Settlement Agreement for Tract 8

The purpose of this Memorandum is to briefly explain the strategic factors that led to the negotiated compensation amount of $ _____ to be paid by the State Department of Roads for the partial taking of 10.0 acres of Tract 8 along the north side of 98th Street.

Several strategic factors led to the final result in this negotiation. First,

Client Memorandum, continued

All of these strategic factors played a role in arriving at the negotiated settlement amount of $ _____. In light of these circumstances, in my judgment the final result was a reasonable resolution of this matter in light of your goals and objectives.

> SUPPLEMENTAL: **Highest and Best Use**

A property's "highest and best use" is a term of art in the appraisal profession. Technically, a property's highest and best use is defined as the reasonably probable and legal use of vacant land or an improved property that is physically possible, appropriately supported, and financially feasible and that results in the highest value. The theoretical emphasis of highest and best use analysis is on the potential uses of the land.

In determining the highest and best use of a property, there are four stages of analysis:

1. *Legally Permissible* - what uses of the property are permitted by zoning, deed restrictions, building codes, historic district controls, and environmental regulations on the site in question?

2. *Physically Possible* - to what uses is it physically possible to put the property in question?

3. *Financially Feasible* - which possible and permissible uses will produce a net return to the owner of the site?

4. *Maximally Productive* - among the financially feasible uses, which use will be maximally productive and offer the highest net return to the owner of the site?

The highest and best use of the site if vacant and available for any use may be different from the current use of the property. In this situation, appraisal theory determines the market value of the property based on its highest and best use and not the property's current use. Tract 8 involves a classic dispute over what is the "highest and best use" of the land. Here, the determination of the highest and best use of the grass pastureland will determine the market value of this portion of Tract 8.

> SUPPLEMENTAL: **Appraisal Theory and Practice**

In disputes over the compensation amount due to a property owner whose land is taken for public use, the private landowner usually consults with a professional real estate appraiser. The landowner may engage the appraiser to prepare a written report explaining the appraiser's analysis and conclusion of market value. If the dispute results in litigation, the appraiser is likely to become an expert witness. If the appraiser becomes an expert witness, the appraiser's written report becomes part of the evidence presented at trial. The governmental entity that is taking the owner's land likewise may engage a professional real estate appraiser as an expert witness. In a litigation battle of dueling expert appraisers, the opposing side attempts to impeach both the analytical process the appraiser used to arrive at a conclusion of market value and the professional credentials and experience of the appraiser.

The Appraisal Process

An appraisal is an opinion of market value. Market value is defined as:

> the most probable price, as of a specified date, in cash, or in terms equivalent to cash, or in other precisely revealed terms, for which the specified property rights should sell after reasonable exposure in a competitive market under all conditions requisite to a fair sale, with the buyer and seller each acting prudently, knowledgeably, and for self-interest, and assuming that neither is under undue duress.[1]

The appraisal process is an analytical format used to estimate market value. Three approaches are used for value estimation. These approaches are known as the Cost Approach, the Sales Comparison Approach and the Income Approach. All three approaches are not necessarily applicable for every property. In addition, all three approaches may have differing degrees of relevance or validity for the property being appraised.

---

1 The Appraisal Institute, *The Appraisal of Real Estate*, 23 (13th ed. 2008).

The **Cost Approach** takes the estimated value of the underlying land and then adds the cost to build a new replacement structure that is similar in size and quality to the existing structure. An allowance for depreciation is subtracted from this amount to reflect the age of the improvements. The Cost Approach is the most applicable for a new or relatively new building where the replacement cost can be estimated with reliability.

The **Sales Comparison Approach** compares the property being appraised with other recently sold properties that possess similar or reasonably adjustable physical characteristics. The Sales Comparison Approach is the most relevant method for estimating market value when similar properties for comparison purposes recently have been sold.

The **Income Approach** is based upon the investment return likely to be generated by the property. Under the Income Approach, the appraiser determines the property's annual net income assuming that the property is rented by an investor-owner. The annual net income is then capitalized to determine the present value of the property. The Income Approach is the most relevant method for a property that would be purchased and rented out by an investor.

Each approach generates a value for the subject property. The appraiser considers the validity of each approach and concludes a final market value for the subject property.

In appraising Tract 8, an appraiser would use only the Sales Comparison Approach. Tract 8 is vacant land without improvements and is not being leased out by Fred Farmer. Therefore, the Cost Approach and the Income Approach are not relevant for determining the market value of Tract 8. But if the 98th Street improvement project involved the taking of a neighborhood retail center, then the Cost and Income Approaches would be highly relevant in determining the value of the owner's property.

The Appraisal Profession

Two independent entities, the Appraisal Institute and the International Right of Way Association, have long provided professional designations to those members who satisfy the organization's educational, examination, and peer-reviewed experience requirements. As a result of federal legislation enacted in response to the savings and loan financial crisis of the late 1980s, individual states began licensing and regulating real estate appraisers in a manner similar to real estate brokers and agents.

The Appraisal Institute provides two professional designations, the MAI and the SRA. The MAI and SRA designations have long been recognized by courts, governmental entities, financial institutions and investors as a mark of significant professional accomplishment in the appraisal field. Appraisers who hold the MAI designation are experienced in the valuation and evaluation of commercial, industrial, residential and special purpose properties. Appraisers who hold the SRA designation are experienced in the valuation of individual residential properties.

The International Right of Way Association offers a series of professional desig-nations. The most prestigious designation is the SR/WA (Senior Right of Way Profes-sional). Real estate appraisers who hold the SR/WA designation specialize in the appraisal of temporary, permanent, partial and complete takings of property for right of way purposes. Like the MAI designation, the SR/WA designation is widely recognized by the courts and governmental entities as a mark of professional achievement in the appraisal field.

In terms of rigor, the state-operated licensing system for real estate appraisers is less demanding than the professional designation programs operated by the Appraisal Institute and the International Right of Way Association. Individual states generally offer two licensing options, a general license and a residential license. A trainee license can be obtained by completing a specified number of classroom educational hours. After a trainee's license is acquired, the trainee may work in the appraisal field. After accumulating one to three years of experience (depending on the type of license and the particular state), the trainee may apply for and receive a permanent state license.

When shopping for a real estate appraiser, the client may prefer to hire the individual who submits the lowest bid for the appraisal work. If a dispute arises over the value of the property, however, the matter may not settle. If a trial is held to determine the value of the property being taken, the professional credentials of the appraiser are an important factor to consider when evaluating whether the appraiser can serve as a persuasive expert witness for your client.

Appendix A

Selected Provisions of the Model Rules of Professional Conduct

▶ RULE 1.0   Terminology

(a) ***"Belief"*** or ***"believes"*** denotes that the person involved actually supposed the fact in question to be true. A person's belief may be inferred from circumstances.

(b) ***"Confirmed in writing,"*** when used in reference to the informed consent of a person, denotes informed consent that is given in writing by the person or a writing that a lawyer promptly transmits to the person confirming an oral informed consent. See paragraph (e) for the definition of "informed consent." If it is not feasible to obtain or transmit the writing at the time the person gives informed consent, then the lawyer must obtain or transmit it within a reasonable time thereafter.

(c) ***"Firm"*** or ***"law firm"*** denotes a lawyer or lawyers in a law partnership, professional corporation, sole proprietorship or other association authorized to practice law, or lawyers employed in a legal services organization or the legal department of a corporation or other organization.

(d) ***"Fraud"*** or ***"fraudulent"*** denotes conduct that is fraudulent under the substantive or procedural law of the applicable jurisdiction and has a purpose to deceive.

(e) ***"Informed consent"*** denotes the agreement by a person to a proposed course of conduct after the lawyer has communicated adequate information and explanation about the material risks of and reasonably available alternatives to the proposed course of conduct.

(f) ***"Knowingly,"*** *"known,"* or ***"knows"*** denotes actual knowledge of the fact in question. A person's knowledge may be inferred from circumstances.

(g) ***"Partner"*** denotes a member of a partnership, a shareholder in a law firm organized as a professional corporation, or a member of an association authorized to practice law.

(h) *"Reasonable"* or *"reasonably"* when used in relation to conduct by a lawyer denotes the conduct of a reasonably prudent and competent lawyer.

(i) *"Reasonable belief"* or *"reasonably believes"* when used in reference to a lawyer denotes that the lawyer believes the matter in question and that the circumstances are such that the belief is reasonable.

(j) *"Reasonably should know"* when used in reference to a lawyer denotes that a lawyer of reasonable prudence and competence would ascertain the matter in question.

(k) *"Screened"* denotes the isolation of a lawyer from any participation in a matter through the timely imposition of procedures within a firm that are reasonably adequate under the circumstances to protect information that the isolated lawyer is obligated to protect under these Rules or other law.

(l) *"Substantial"* when used in reference to degree or extent denotes a material matter of clear and weighty importance.

(m) *"Tribunal"* denotes a court, an arbitrator in a binding arbitration proceeding or a legislative body, administrative agency or other body acting in an adjudicative capacity. A legislative body, administrative agency or other body acts in an adjudicative capacity when a neutral official, after the presentation of evidence or legal argument by a party or parties, will render a binding legal judgment directly affecting a party's interests in a particular matter.

(n) *"Writing"* or *"written"* denotes a tangible or electronic record of a communication or representation, including handwriting, typewriting, printing, photostating, photography, audio or video recording and e-mail. A writing includes an electronic sound, symbol or process attached to or logically associated with a writing and executed or adopted by a person with the intent to sign the writing.

▶ RULE 1.1 Competence

A lawyer shall provide competent representation to a client. Competent representation requires the legal knowledge, skill, thoroughness and preparation reasonably necessary for the representation.

▶ Rule 1.2 Scope of Representation and Allocation of Authority between Client and Lawyer

(a) Subject to paragraphs (c) and (d), a lawyer shall abide by a client's decisions concerning the objectives of representation and, as required by Rule 1.4, shall consult with the client as to the means by which they are to be pursued. A lawyer may take such action on behalf of the client as is impliedly authorized to carry out the representation. A lawyer shall abide by a client's decision whether to settle a matter. In a criminal case, the lawyer shall abide by the client's decision, after consultation with the lawyer, as to a plea to be entered, whether to waive jury trial and whether the client will testify.

(b) A lawyer's representation of a client, including representation by appointment, does not constitute an endorsement of the client's political, economic, social or moral views or activities.

(c) A lawyer may limit the scope of the representation if the limitation is reasonable under the circumstances and the client gives informed consent.

(d) A lawyer shall not counsel a client to engage, or assist a client, in conduct that the lawyer knows is criminal or fraudulent, but a lawyer may discuss the legal consequences of any proposed course of conduct with a client and may counsel or assist a client to make a good faith effort to determine the validity, scope, meaning or application of the law.

* * *

▶ RULE 1.4 Communication

(a) A lawyer shall:

(1) promptly inform the client of any decision or circumstance with respect to which the client's informed consent, as defined in Rule 1.0(e), is required by these Rules;

(2) reasonably consult with the client about the means by which the client's objectives are to be accomplished;

(3) keep the client reasonably informed about the status of the matter;

(4) promptly comply with reasonable requests for information; and

(5) consult with the client about any relevant limitation on the lawyer's conduct when the lawyer knows that the client expects assistance not permitted by the Rules of Professional Conduct or other law.

(b) A lawyer shall explain a matter to the extent reasonably necessary to permit the client to make informed decisions regarding the representation.

▶ RULE 1.5 Fees

(a) A lawyer shall not make an agreement for, charge, or collect an unreasonable fee or an unreasonable amount for expenses. The factors to be considered in determining the reasonableness of a fee include the following:

(1) the time and labor required, the novelty and difficulty of the questions involved, and the skill requisite to perform the legal service properly;

(2) the likelihood, if apparent to the client, that the acceptance of the particular employment will preclude other employment by the lawyer;

(3) the fee customarily charged in the locality for similar legal services;

(4) the amount involved and the results obtained;

(5) the time limitations imposed by the client or by the circumstances;

(6) the nature and length of the professional relationship with the client;

(7) the experience, reputation, and ability of the lawyer or lawyers performing the services; and

(8) whether the fee is fixed or contingent.

(b) The scope of the representation and the basis or rate of the fee and expenses for which the client will be responsible shall be communicated to the client, preferably in writing, before or within a reasonable time after commencing the representation, except when the lawyer will charge a regularly represented client on the same basis or rate. Any changes in the basis or rate of the fee or expenses shall also be communicated to the client.

(c) A fee may be contingent on the outcome of the matter for which the service is rendered, except in a matter in which a contingent fee is prohibited by paragraph (d) or other law. A contingent fee agreement shall be in a writing signed by the client and shall state the method by which the fee is to be determined, including the percentage or percentages that shall accrue to the lawyer in the event of settlement, trial or appeal; litigation and other expenses to be deducted from the recovery; and whether such expenses are to be deducted before or after the contingent fee is calculated. The agreement must clearly notify the client of any expenses for which the client will be liable whether or not the client is the prevailing party. Upon conclusion of a contingent fee matter, the lawyer shall provide the client with a written statement stating the outcome of the matter and, if there is a recovery, showing the remittance to the client and the method of its determination.

(d) A lawyer shall not enter into an arrangement for, charge, or collect:

(1) any fee in a domestic relations matter, the payment or amount of which is contingent upon the securing of a divorce or upon the amount of alimony or support, or property settlement in lieu thereof; or

(2) a contingent fee for representing a defendant in a criminal case.

(e) A division of a fee between lawyers who are not in the same firm may be made only if:

(1) the division is in proportion to the services performed by each lawyer or each lawyer assumes joint responsibility for the representation;

(2) the client agrees to the arrangement, including the share each lawyer will receive, and the agreement is confirmed in writing; and

(3) the total fee is reasonable.

▶ RULE 1.6 Confidentiality of Information

(a) A lawyer shall not reveal information relating to the representation of a client unless the client gives informed consent, the disclosure is impliedly authorized in order to carry out the representation or the disclosure is permitted by paragraph (b).

(b) A lawyer may reveal information relating to the representation of a client to the extent the lawyer reasonably believes necessary:

(1) to prevent reasonably certain death or substantial bodily harm;

(2) to prevent the client from committing a crime or fraud that is reasonably certain to result in substantial injury to the financial interests or property of another and in furtherance of which the client has used or is using the lawyer's services;

(3) to prevent, mitigate or rectify substantial injury to the financial interests or property of another that is reasonably certain to result or has resulted from the client's commission of a crime or fraud in furtherance of which the client has used the lawyer's services;

(4) to secure legal advice about the lawyer's compliance with these Rules;

(5) to establish a claim or defense on behalf of the lawyer in a controversy between the lawyer and the client, to establish a

defense to a criminal charge or civil claim against the lawyer based upon conduct in which the client was involved, or to respond to allegations in any proceeding concerning the lawyer's representation of the client; or

(6) to comply with other law or a court order.

▶ RULE 1.7 Conflict of Interest: Current Clients

(a) Except as provided in paragraph (b), a lawyer shall not represent a client if the representation involves a concurrent conflict of interest. Concurrent conflict of interest exists if:

(1) the representation of one client will be directly adverse to another client; or

(2) there is a significant risk that the representation of one or more clients will be materially limited by the lawyer's responsibilities to another client, a former client or a third person or by a personal interest of the lawyer.

(b) Notwithstanding the existence of a concurrent conflict of interest under paragraph (a), a lawyer may represent a client if:

(1) the lawyer reasonably believes that the lawyer will be able to provide competent and diligent representation to each affected client;

(2) the representation is not prohibited by law;

(3) the representation does not involve the assertion of a claim by one client against another client represented by the lawyer in the same litigation or other proceeding before a tribunal; and

(4) each affected client gives informed consent, confirmed in writing.

* * *

▶ Rule 1.13   Organization as Client

(a) A lawyer employed or retained by an organization represents the organization acting through its duly authorized constituents.

(b) If a lawyer for an organization knows that an officer, employee or other person associated with the organization is engaged in action, intends to act or refuses to act in a matter related to the representation that is a violation of a legal obligation to the organization, or a violation of law that reasonably might be imputed to the organization, and that is likely to result in substantial injury to the organization, then the lawyer shall proceed as is reasonably necessary in the best interest of the organization. Unless the lawyer reasonably believes that it is not necessary in the best interest of the organization to do so, the lawyer shall refer the matter to higher authority in the organization, including, if warranted by the circumstances, to the highest authority that can act on behalf of the organization as determined by applicable law.

(c) Except as provided in paragraph (d), if

(1) despite the lawyer's efforts in accordance with paragraph (b) the highest authority that can act on behalf of the organization insists upon or fails to address in a timely and appropriate manner an action, or a refusal to act, that is clearly a violation of law, and

(2) the lawyer reasonably believes that the violation is reasonably certain to result in substantial injury to the organization, then the lawyer may reveal information relating to the representation whether or not Rule 1.6 permits such disclosure, but only if and to the extent the lawyer reasonably

believes necessary to prevent substantial injury to the organization.

(d) Paragraph (c) shall not apply with respect to information relating to a lawyer's representation of an organization to investigate an alleged violation of law, or to defend the organization or an officer, employee or other constituent associated with the organization against a claim arising out of an alleged violation of law.

(e) A lawyer who reasonably believes that he or she has been discharged because of the lawyer's actions taken pursuant to paragraphs (b) or (c), or who withdraws under circumstances that require or permit the lawyer to take action under either of those paragraphs, shall proceed as the lawyer reasonably believes necessary to assure that the organization's highest authority is informed of the lawyer's discharge or withdrawal.

(f) In dealing with an organization's directors, officers, employees, members, shareholders or other constituents, a lawyer shall explain the identity of the client when the lawyer knows or reasonably should know that the organization's interests are adverse to those of the constituents with whom the lawyer is dealing.

(g) A lawyer representing an organization may also represent any of its directors, officers, employees, members, shareholders or other consti-tuents, subject to the provisions of Rule 1.7. If the organization's consent to the dual representation is required by Rule 1.7, the consent shall be given by an appropriate official of the organization other than the individual who is to be represented, or by the shareholders.

* * *

▶ Rule 1.14   Client with Diminished Capacity

(a) When a client's capacity to make adequately considered decisions in connection with a representation is diminished, whether because of minority, mental impairment or for some other reason, the lawyer shall, as far as reasonably possible, maintain a normal client-lawyer relationship with the client.

(b) When the lawyer reasonably believes that the client has diminished capacity, is at risk of substantial physical, financial or other harm unless action is taken and cannot adequately act in the client's own interest, the lawyer may take reasonably necessary protective action, including consulting with individuals or entities that have the ability to take action to protect the client and, in appropriate cases, seeking the appointment of a guardian ad litem, conservator or guardian.

(c) Information relating to the representation of a client with diminished capacity is protected by Rule 1.6. When taking protective action pursuant to paragraph (b), the lawyer is impliedly authorized under Rule 1.6(a) to reveal information about the client, but only to the extent reasonably necessary to protect the client's interests.

* * *

▶ RULE 1.16   Declining or Terminating Representation

(a) Except as stated in paragraph (c), a lawyer shall not represent a client or, where representation has commenced, shall withdraw from the representation of a client if:

(1) the representation will result in violation of the Rules of Professional Conduct or other law;

(2) the lawyer's physical or mental condition materially impairs the lawyer's ability to represent the client; or

(3) the lawyer is discharged.

(b) Except as stated in paragraph (c), a lawyer may withdraw from representing a client if:

(1) withdrawal can be accomplished without material adverse effect on the interests of the client;

(2) the client persists in a course of action involving the lawyer's services that the lawyer reasonably believes is criminal or fraudulent;

(3) the client has used the lawyer's services to perpetrate a crime or fraud;

(4) the client insists upon taking action that the lawyer considers repugnant or with which the lawyer has a fundamental disagreement;

(5) the client fails substantially to fulfill an obligation to the lawyer regarding the lawyer's services and has been given reasonable warning that the lawyer will withdraw unless the obligation is fulfilled;

(6) the representation will result in an unreasonable financial burden on the lawyer or has been rendered unreasonably difficult by the client; or

(7) other good cause for withdrawal exists.

(c) A lawyer must comply with applicable law requiring notice to or permission of a tribunal when terminating a representation. When ordered to do so by a tribunal, a lawyer shall continue representation notwithstanding good cause for terminating the representation.

(d) Upon termination of representation, a lawyer shall take steps to the extent reasonably practicable to protect a client's interests, such as giving reasonable notice to the client, allowing time for employment of other counsel, surrendering papers and property to which the client is entitled and refunding any advance payment of fee or expense that has not been earned or incurred. The lawyer may retain papers relating to the client to the extent permitted by other law.

* * *

▶ RULE 2.1   Advisor

In representing a client, a lawyer shall exercise independent professional judgment and render candid advice. In rendering advice, a lawyer may refer not only to law but to other considerations such as moral, economic, social and political factors, that may be relevant to the client's situation.

* * *

▶ RULE 3.1   Meritorious Claims and Contentions

A lawyer shall not bring or defend a proceeding, or assert or controvert an issue therein, unless there is a basis in law and fact for doing so that is not frivolous, which includes a good faith argument for an extension, modification or reversal of existing law. A lawyer for the defendant in a criminal proceeding, or the respondent in a proceeding that could result in incarceration, may nevertheless so defend the proceeding as to require that every element of the case be established.

* * *

▶ RULE 3.3   Candor Toward the Tribunal

(a) A lawyer shall not knowingly:

(1) make a false statement of fact or law to a tribunal or fail to correct a false statement of material fact or law previously made to the tribunal by the lawyer;

(2) fail to disclose to the tribunal legal authority in the controlling jurisdiction known to the lawyer to be directly adverse to the position of the client and not disclosed by opposing counsel; or

(3) offer evidence that the lawyer knows to be false. If a lawyer, the lawyer's client, or a witness called by the lawyer, has offered material evidence and the lawyer comes to know of its falsity, the lawyer shall take reasonable remedial measures, including, if necessary, disclosure to the tribunal. A lawyer may refuse to offer evidence, other than the testimony of a defendant in a criminal matter, that the lawyer reasonably believes is false.

(b) A lawyer who represents a client in an adjudicative proceeding and who knows that a person intends to engage, is engaging or has engaged in criminal or fraudulent conduct related to the proceeding shall take reasonable remedial measures, including, if necessary, disclosure to the tribunal.

(c) The duties stated in paragraphs (a) and (b) continue to the conclusion of the proceeding, and apply even if compliance requires disclosure of information otherwise protected by Rule 1.6.

(d) In an ex parte proceeding, a lawyer shall inform the tribunal of all material facts known to the lawyer that will enable the tribunal to make an informed decision, whether or not the facts are adverse.

▶ RULE 3.4 Fairness to Opposing Party and Counsel

A lawyer shall not:

(a) unlawfully obstruct another party's access to evidence or unlawfully alter, destroy or conceal a document or other material having potential evidentiary value. A lawyer shall not counsel or assist another person to do any such act;

(b) falsify evidence, counsel or assist a witness to testify falsely, or offer an inducement to a witness that is prohibited by law;

(c) knowingly disobey an obligation under the rules of a tribunal, except for an open refusal based on an assertion that no valid obligation exists;

(d) in pretrial procedure, make a frivolous discovery request or fail to make reasonably diligent effort to comply with a legally proper discovery request by an opposing party;

(e) in trial, allude to any matter that the lawyer does not reasonably believe is relevant or that will not be supported by admissible evidence, assert personal knowledge of facts in issue except when testifying as a witness, or state a personal opinion as to the justness of a cause, the credibility of a witness, the culpability of a civil litigant or the guilt or innocence of an accused; or

(f) request a person other than a client to refrain from voluntarily giving relevant information to another party unless:

(1) the person is a relative or an employee or other agent of a client; and

(2) the lawyer reasonably believes that the person's interests will not be adversely affected by refraining from giving such information.

▶ RULE 4.1   Truthfulness in Statements to Others

In the course of representing a client a lawyer shall not knowingly:

(a) make a false statement of material fact or law to a third person; or

(b) fail to disclose a material fact when disclosure is necessary to avoid assisting a criminal or fraudulent act by a client, unless disclosure is prohibited by Rule 1.6.

▶ RULE 4.3   Dealing with Unrepresented Person

In dealing on behalf of a client with a person who is not represented by counsel, a lawyer shall not state or imply that the lawyer is disinterested. When the lawyer knows or reasonably should know that the unrepresented person misunderstands the lawyer's role in the matter, the lawyer shall make reasonable efforts to correct the misunderstanding. The lawyer shall not give legal advice to an unrepresented person, other than the advice to secure counsel, if the lawyer knows or reasonably should know that the interests of such a person are or have a reasonable possibility of being in conflict with the interests of the client.

▶ Rule 5.1   Responsibilities of Partners, Managers, and Supervisory Lawyers

(a) A partner in a law firm, and a lawyer who individually or together with other lawyers possesses comparable managerial authority in a law firm, shall make reasonable efforts to ensure that the firm has in effect measures giving reasonable assurance that all lawyers in the firm conform to the Rules of Professional Conduct.

(b) A lawyer having direct supervisory authority over another lawyer shall make reasonable efforts to ensure that the other lawyer conforms to the Rules of Professional Conduct.

(c) A lawyer shall be responsible for another lawyer's violation of the Rules of Professional Conduct if:

(1) the lawyer orders or, with knowledge of the specific conduct, ratifies the conduct involved; or

(2) the lawyer is a partner or has comparable managerial authority in the law firm in which the other lawyer practices, or has direct supervisory authority over the other lawyer, and knows of the conduct at a time when its consequences can be avoided or mitigated but fails to take reasonable remedial action.

▶ Rule 5.2   Responsibilities of a Subordinate Lawyer

(a) A lawyer is bound by the Rules of Professional Conduct notwithstanding that the lawyer acted at the direction of another person.

(b) A subordinate lawyer does not violate the Rules of Professional Conduct if that lawyer acts in accordance with a supervisory lawyer's reasonable resolution of an arguable question of professional duty.

* * *

▶ RULE 5.4   Professional Independence of a Lawyer

(a) A lawyer or law firm shall not share legal fees with a nonlawyer, except that:

(1) an agreement by a lawyer with the lawyer's firm, partner, or associate may provide for the payment of money, over a reasonable period of time after the lawyer's death, to the lawyer's estate or to one or more specified persons;

(2) a lawyer who purchases the practice of a deceased, disabled, or disappeared lawyer may, pursuant to the provisions of Rule 1.17, pay to the estate or other representative of that lawyer the agreed-upon purchase price;

(3) a lawyer or law firm may include nonlawyer employees in a compensation or retirement plan, even though the plan is based in whole or in part on a profit-sharing arrangement; and

(4) a lawyer may share court-awarded legal fees with a nonprofit organization that employed, retained or recommended employment of the lawyer in the matter.

▶ RULE 8.3 Reporting Professional Misconduct

(a) A lawyer who knows that another lawyer has committed a violation of the Rules of Professional Conduct that raises a substantial question as to that lawyer's honesty, trustworthiness or fitness as a lawyer in other respects, shall inform the appropriate professional authority.

(b) A lawyer who knows that a judge has committed a violation of applicable rules of judicial conduct that raises a substantial question as to the judge's fitness for office shall inform the appropriate authority.

(c) This Rule does not require disclosure of information otherwise protected by Rule 1.6 or information gained by a lawyer or judge while participating in an approved lawyers assistance program.

▶ RULE 8.4 Misconduct

It is professional misconduct for a lawyer to:

(a) violate or attempt to violate the Rules of Professional Conduct, knowingly assist or induce another to do so, or do so through the acts of another;

(b) commit a criminal act that reflects adversely on the lawyer's honesty, trustworthiness or fitness as a lawyer in other respects;

(c) engage in conduct involving dishonesty, fraud, deceit or misrepresentation;

(d) engage in conduct that is prejudicial to the administration of justice;

(e) state or imply an ability to influence improperly a government agency or official or to achieve results by means that violate the Rules of Professional Conduct or other law; or

(f) knowingly assist a judge or judicial officer in conduct that is a violation of applicable rules of judicial conduct or other law.

Time Sheet Entry

Attorney Name:

Client: Billing No.:

DATE	DESCRIPTION	TIME

Time Sheet Entry

Attorney Name:

Client: Billing No.:

DATE	DESCRIPTION	TIME

Time Sheet Entry

Attorney Name:

Client: Billing No.:

DATE	DESCRIPTION	TIME

Time Sheet Entry

Attorney Name:

Client: Billing No.:

DATE	DESCRIPTION	TIME

Time Sheet Entry

Attorney Name:

Client: Billing No.:

DATE	DESCRIPTION	TIME

Time Sheet Entry

Attorney Name:

Client: Billing No.:

DATE	DESCRIPTION	TIME

Time Sheet Entry

Attorney Name:

Client: Billing No.:

DATE	DESCRIPTION	TIME

Time Sheet Entry

Attorney Name:

Client: Billing No.:

DATE	DESCRIPTION	TIME

Time Sheet Entry

Attorney Name:

Client: Billing No.:

DATE	DESCRIPTION	TIME

Time Sheet Entry

Attorney Name:

Client: Billing No.:

DATE	DESCRIPTION	TIME

Time Sheet Entry

Attorney Name:

Client: Billing No.:

DATE	DESCRIPTION	TIME

Time Sheet Entry

Attorney Name:

Client: Billing No.:

DATE	DESCRIPTION	TIME